WORLD CATASTROPHE: BEHOLD HE COMETH

by

Rhodalee Malone Hailey

Ronald A. Ralph

WORLD CATASTROPHE: BEHOLD HE COMETH
by Rhodalee Malone Hailey and Ronald A. Ralph

ISBN 978-0-9792562-9-5
0-9792562-9-1

Cover design by Marlene Tascarella

Published by Victory Baptist Press
Milton, Florida – USA

www.victorybaptistpress.com

Dedicated to

Any and all who read and heed its message.

Acknowledgements

I wish to acknowledge my appreciation to my sister, Willard Hetsch, for her patience and help in proofreading this material, and to my friend, Francis Evans, for her encouragement and help in getting it published.

Preface

"O the depth of the riches both of the wisdom and knowledge of God! how unsearchable are his judgments, and his ways past finding out!" (Romans 11:33)

In 1988 I met a retired school teacher who I can now say became one of the greatest influences in my life and ministry. The teacher was Mrs. Rhodalee Malone Hailey. When I first met Mrs. Hailey, I was a young preacher and would have never guessed that God would use this "elderly lady" to make such an impact on my life. The events of the next several years and my time in prayer and discussion with Mrs. Hailey would remind me over and over again that truly, God's ways are past finding out! I soon discovered two things about Mrs. Hailey that still challenge me to this day. First, she was one of the few prayer warriors that I have ever met and second, she was a very diligent student of the word of God.

Mrs. Hailey went to be with the Lord in 1995, but I sincerely believe that I am still reaping some of the benefits of her prayers! In fact, one of the faithful men of our church was saved in a public school classroom in the 1960s as Mrs. Hailey led him to the Lord!!

Concerning her prayer life, Mrs. Hailey spent much time alone with God. After she departed this life, I was given many of her Bible study notes, poems, songs, and prayer journals. As I browsed those journals I was brought to tears as I saw the names of so many people she prayed for. She prayed for young children, teenagers, missionaries and many others. One of the amazing things was the list of pastors she prayed for; almost every pastor in our town was on her list, including me!!! Alongside all the names were many notes, information about each person, answers to prayers, and burdens of her heart. I will repeat myself and tell you again, I am convinced that her prayers are still being answered and that I am enjoying fruit to her account!

As for Mrs. Hailey's time in the word of God, I'll relate one story. She was a Sunday School teacher when I first became her pastor. On Sunday nights, I would teach our teachers the lesson which they would teach their class on the following Sunday. I gave all the teachers my typed notes and they would use the material as a starting point for their lesson. Along with all the prayer journals and items I received upon her death were many of those lessons, with all of her added notes, questions, and references. Now my lessons are much better!!! I was shocked and thrilled to see how much time she had given to each lesson.

Mrs. Hailey asked me several times to edit or co-author this book. The book is really hers and my part is very small. I consented to do some editing and make a few changes and additions primarily to honor her request and to attempt to get this book in circulation. I believe Mrs. Hailey's approach to Revelation and her style in writing will appeal to an audience that might otherwise avoid such a book. My prayer is that this book will extend even more, Mrs. Hailey's labor of love and also be a blessing to all who read it.

–Pastor Ron Ralph

Foreword

When, in the fall of the year, we see the sap-starved, color laden leaves, loosed from their moorings, go swirling through the air to their appointed doom, we know that winter is near. There is no mistaking the signs, for God has set the seasons in their courses and they have never failed, according to His promise that "While the earth remaineth, seedtime and harvest, and cold and heat, and summer and winter, and day and night shall not cease" (Genesis 8:22).

Even so, God has a timetable for the rise and fall of Gentile world power, with signs accompanying, and the blood-stained, sin-laden pages from the ledger of current events blowing in the winds of adversity are ominous harbingers of the approaching season of doom for our present world system.

Jesus sternly rebuked the Jewish leaders for being able to predict rain and heat by the drift of the clouds, yet could not discern the time in which they were living. Addressing them as hypocrites, He reprimanded them for their utter lack of awareness of the presence of the Messiah in their midst.

"*Ye* hypocrites," He quipped, "Ye can discern the face of the sky and of the earth, but how is it that ye do not discern this time?" (Luke 12:56).

Today we have a backdrop of signals from the beginning of world history, down to the present day, to warn us of the dire consequences which come to peoples and nations that forget God and scorn His commandments.

The Roman, Grecian, Media-Persian, Assyrian and Babylonian Empires all became vulnerable to outside forces because of internal rottenness and decay. The pattern is ever the same, a general forsaking of God's guidance and a flagrant replacing of His immutable laws with the fluctuating logic of man's reasoning. From there on, the course is down, down, down, and judgment is the only alternative.

Going back to Old Testament days, we find numerous instances where God used cataclysmic upheavals in nature for purposes of judgment upon sinful, rebellious mankind.

It was God who sent the floodwaters of destruction upon the earth in the days of Noah, and caused only eight persons to be saved out of all living souls (Genesis 6:5–13). It was He who rained fire and brimstone upon Sodom and Gomorrah for their sins of fornication and homosexuality (Jude 7 with Genesis 19:24).

It was God who sent the plagues upon the Egyptians for oppressing His people, Israel, and later drowned the whole Egyptian army in the Red Sea. It was He who made the earth to swallow alive Korah and his followers, together with their homes and families for opposing His servant, Moses (Numbers 16:31–33).

It was God who visited the children of Israel with thunder and earthquake, with storm and tempest, and the flame of devouring fire, who sent the sword, the famine, the pestilence and the heathen to punish them for going after other gods and refusing to heed His commandments (Isaiah 29:6).

It is God who promises to, once again, pour out His wrath upon this wicked, God-rejecting world, and to rid it of all impurities and all iniquity in preparation for His coming King and Kingdom.

“Because he hath appointed a day, in which he will judge the world in righteousness by *that* man [Jesus Christ] whom he hath ordained … who shall judge the quick and the dead at his appearing” (Acts 17:31; 2 Timothy 4:1).

God’s word has gone out concerning our Godless generation. Civilization is headed for a coup d’e tat with destiny! The conflagration is at hand, even at the doors!

Contents

Chapter 1
BEHOLD HE COMETH

Repent! Repent! Repent!

> "... be zealous therefore, and repent" (Revelation 3:19).

> "Repent ye therefore, and be converted ..." (Acts 3:19).

> "Repent: for the kingdom of heaven is at hand" (Matthew 4:17).

Once again, God's call to repentance is sounding a dire warning to all mankind—to Jew, to Gentile, to Catholic, to Protestant, to you and to me—to every living soul upon the face of the earth. Again, it is heralding the news of the coming **King** and **His Kingdom**:

> "The voice of him that crieth in the wilderness, Prepare ye the way of the LORD, make straight in the desert a highway for our God. Every valley shall be exalted, and every mountain and hill shall be made low: and the crooked shall be made straight, and the rough places plain: And the glory of the LORD shall be revealed,

and all flesh shall see *it* together: for the mouth of the LORD hath spoken *it*" (Isaiah 40:3–5).

"Behold, the Lord cometh with ten thousands of his saints, To execute judgment upon all …" (Jude 1:14, 15).

"… then shall he sit upon the throne of his glory: And before him shall be gathered all nations: and he shall separate them one from another, as a shepherd divideth *his* sheep from the goats" (Matthew 25:31, 32).

"And the LORD shall be king over all the earth: in that day shall there be one LORD, and his name one" (Zechariah 14:9).

Down through the centuries of world events come these illustrious, prophetic voices blending into one clear and perfect note, laden with **awe** and **expectancy**. In one breath, as it were, they proclaim the imminent, personal **return of Christ** to earth, the accompanying **judgment** upon a wicked, Christ-rejecting world, and the **universal peace** and **glory** which shall follow:

"Behold, he cometh with clouds; and every eye shall see him, and they *also* which pierced him: and all kindreds of the earth shall wail because of him. Even so, Amen" (Revelation 1:7).

"Behold, I will send my messenger, and he shall prepare the way before me: and the Lord, whom ye seek, shall suddenly come to his temple ... behold, he shall come, saith the LORD of hosts" (Malachi 3:1).

"For as the lightning cometh out of the east, and shineth even unto the west; so shall also the coming of the Son of man be" (Matthew 24:27).

"For yet a little while, and he that shall come will come, and will not tarry" (Hebrews 10:37).

Yes, the **Lord Jesus Christ**, the **Son of God,** and the **Saviour** of the world is soon to make a second appearance upon the earth just as literally and personally as He made His first appearance as the Babe of Bethlehem almost 2,000 years ago. But this time He will come, not as the meek and lowly servant of mankind to be denied, reviled, and persecuted, but He will appear in all of the **glory and splendor** of the **heavenly regalia**, executing **judgment** upon a Christ-rejecting world, and taking His rightful place as **King of Kings** and **Lord of Lords**.

Unfortunately, the **second coming of Christ** and the life beyond have been **spiritualized** until they have little meaning for the average person. While we openly criticize and condemn the Jews for being "slow of heart to believe all that the prophets have spoken" (Luke 24:25), concerning the **sufferings** of their Messiah, the greater reproach is ours for being slow of heart to believe all they have spoken concerning His **future glory**.

We readily accept the reality of His first appearance because it is fulfilled prophecy, and historical documents attest to the truth of His life and works. Yet, the Scriptures pertaining to His Second Coming are usually given a spiritual interpretation, which flatly rejects a **personal**, **bodily appearance**.

However, our Lord's return to earth is spoken of in exactly the same terms as His departure. When He was taken up out of sight on a cloud in the presence of His disciples, two angels appeared to them and said: "Ye men of Galilee, why stand ye gazing up into heaven? this same Jesus, which is taken up from you into heaven, shall so come in like manner as ye have seen him go into heaven" (Acts 1:11).

Jesus went to heaven on a cloud in a glorified, visible body, while His disciples stood gazing in utter amazement (Luke 24:50, 51), and He will return in like manner. It will be visible, literal, spectacular, **horrifying**! Every eye will see Him, and all kindreds of the earth will wail (cry out in fear and amazement) because of His sudden appearance.

When we say every eye will see Him, we are speaking of the Lord's **return to the earth**. Before He returns to the earth, He will first call out His church (1 Thessalonians 4:13–18). This rapture will be followed by what is known as the Great Tribulation (Matt. 24), which will last for seven years. It is after the Great Tribulation, which is described in the book of Revelation, that the Lord will return to the earth where "every eye shall see him" (Revelation 1:7).

The purpose of His coming is two-fold: **First**, it is for the pulling down of Satan's strongholds. **Second**, it is for the establishment of His own righteous Kingdom (the kingdom of heaven), over which He will rule with unquestionable authority for 1,000 years.

"… the kingdom of heaven is at hand" (Matthew 3:2; 4:17) was the message proclaimed by both Jesus and John the

Baptist at the beginning of this present age. It is also the message for the close of the age (Daniel 7:13, 14).

Scripturally speaking, the kingdom of heaven is a literal, physical, visible kingdom. When Jesus Christ came the first time, the Jews were expecting Him to conquer Rome and set up this kingdom with the capital in Jerusalem. But He did not do this the first time. His first coming was as King of righteousness, and His second coming will be as King of peace (Hebrews 7:1–2). You might ask why an earthly kingdom would be called "the kingdom of heaven?" Did Jesus not teach his disciples to pray, "Thy kingdom come. Thy will be done in earth, as *it is* in heaven" (Matthew 6:10)? Aren't we all longing for "heaven on earth?"

Concerning Jesus Christ, Gabriel told Mary, "He shall be great, and shall be called the Son of the Highest: and the Lord God shall give unto him the throne of his father David: And he shall reign over the house of Jacob for ever; and of his kingdom there shall be no end" (Luke 1:32, 33). This prophecy has yet to be fulfilled. Jesus Christ has not yet taken the throne of David in Jerusalem, but He is going to! He is going to bring in the kingdom of heaven. Until then, His saints are to be busy serving Him in the "kingdom of God," which is a spiritual kingdom of which the church is a part (Romans 14:17). But never forget, the **King is coming**; and when He does, He will take over both kingdoms and rule and reign forever!

> "Wherefore God also hath highly exalted him, and given him a name which is above every name: That at the name of Jesus every knee should bow, of *things* in heaven, and *things* in earth, and *things* under the

earth; And *that* every tongue should confess that Jesus Christ *is* Lord, to the glory of God the Father" (Philippians 2:9–11).

"For he must reign, till he hath put all enemies under his feet. The last enemy *that* shall be destroyed *is* death" (1 Corinthians 15:25, 26). (See also Malachi 4:1--3; Matthew 24:29–31; Revelation 20:1–4.)

Chapter 2
END TIME EVENTS

Three great, earth-shattering events will characterize the return of Christ in glory to bring to an end this dispensation of the age of grace and Gentile world rule.

RAPTURE OF THE REDEEMED

First, the **Rapture of the Redeemed** must occur, for God has promised deliverance to all who look for Him and love His appearing (Hebrews 9:28; Revelation 3:10).

This will be a time of ecstasy for the New Testament body of believers, both dead and alive, when Christ suddenly descends on a cloud in mid-heaven and catches them out of this sin-infested world, to be forever in His presence (1 Corinthians 15:51–57; 1 Thessalonians 4:16, 17).

There are no signs accompanying this event. No one knows, not even the angels of heaven, the "day" nor the "hour" in which it will take place, but only the Father in heaven (Matthew 24:36). The **Rapture** is imminent—it could happen at any moment!

THE GREAT TRIBULATION

Following close upon the Rapture will be the outbreak of **the Great Tribulation**, first spoken of by Daniel (Daniel 12:1) and reiterated by Jesus in His discourse on end-time events (Matthew 24).

Also called the **Day of the Lord**, this will be a day of "destruction from the Almighty"—"a day of clouds and thick darkness" (Joel 1:15; Zephaniah 1:15), when "the earth shall quake … the heavens shall tremble: the sun and the moon shall be dark, and the stars shall withdraw their shining" (Joel 2:10). So terrible shall that day be, that men will cry out for the mountains and rocks to fall on them, to hide them from the face of God's wrath (Revelation 6:16, 17).

BATTLE OF ARMAGEDDON

After three and one-half years of deceptive peace (Daniel 11:21), followed by three and one-half years of unrelenting human suffering, world history will climax in the third great event, the **Battle of Armageddon**, at which time the glorified Christ will rend the heavens and descend to earth with His mighty armies to complete the clean-up and start a new reign of peace and righteousness (Revelation 19:11–20:3).

Jesus likened the days preceding His return to the days of Noah just before the flood. In that day, the sophisticated populace refused to believe and heed Noah's warnings regarding the oncoming deluge. With renewed emphasis on the social and materialistic aspects of life, they went blithely on their way, buying and selling, building and planting, eating and drinking, marrying and giving in marriage, until the day Noah entered into the ark: "And knew not until the flood came, and took them all away" (Luke 17:27, 28; Matthew 24:39). Foolishly and passionately they sought gratification for their fleshly desires to the neglect of spiritual and eternal verities.

The Genesis record gives a graphic account of the evil conditions which prevailed just preceding the flood and why God was compelled to destroy the bulk of the human race. "And GOD saw that the wickedness of man *was* great in the earth, and *that* every imagination of the thoughts of his heart *was* only evil continually ... The earth also was corrupt before God, and the earth was filled with violence" (Genesis 6:5, 11).

Jesus also likened those days to **Sodom** and **Gomorrah** in the days of Lot, when God rained **fire** and **brimstone** upon them from heaven.

> "Likewise also as it was in the days of Lot; they did eat, they drank, they bought, they sold, they planted, they builded; But the same day that Lot went out of Sodom it rained fire and brimstone from heaven, and destroyed *them* all. Even thus shall it be in the day when the Son of man is revealed" (Luke 17:28–30).

Turning to the book of Jude, we find the reason for their destruction. They were totally given over to the lust of the flesh, fornication and homosexuality being their chief offences (Jude 7).

What a warning to our present generation, which is characterized by such widespread sexual depravity as has not been known since the days of Noah and Lot!

Chapter 3
IMPENDING DESTRUCTION

God's overall purpose is to redeem His creation from the bondage of corruption, which Satan has imposed. But He must first redeem mankind, and this He began to do at Golgotha through the shed blood of "his only begotten Son, that whosoever believeth in him should not perish, but have everlasting life" (John 3:16).

During this present age of grace, God's Holy Spirit is striving with all humanity, calling out a people for His name, purifying them in the fires of affliction, redeeming them for all eternity (Acts 15:14; 1 Corinthians 3:11–15). This process will continue right down to the end of the age, as the earth also undergoes a baptism of fire.

Second Peter 3:7–10 tells us that "the heavens and earth, which are now, by the same word are kept in store, reserved unto fire against the day of judgment and perdition of ungodly men."

This old earth, which rightfully belongs to its Creator (Psalms 24:1), has been invaded by the enemy (Satan), who for over 6,000 years, has wreaked havoc from pole to pole, until the whole creation groans and travails under the burden of the curse, seeking deliverance from the bondage of corruption (Romans 8:20–22).

When Jesus was questioned concerning the signs that would precede His return, He listed a number of things, including war, famine, pestilences, earthquakes, afflictions, betrayals, signs in the heavens, distresses of nations, false christs and false prophets. Labeling these "the beginning of sorrows," He then concluded with the statement, "... this gospel of the kingdom shall be preached in all the world for a witness unto all nations; and then shall the end come" (Matthew 24:14).

Today, the message of God's saving grace is going out into all the world as never before in the history of man. Evangelical groups are making the greatest concerted effort of all time to get the Gospel message out to the whole world. Radio and television, coupled with the amazing satellite, have opened up a whole new field of communication, so that people of every nation and tribe are hearing the Gospel for the first time in their own languages. But according to God's Word, the great majority of the populace will continue to reject His Son, Jesus, who alone can give them life eternal,[1] and Gentile world rule will phase out during a period of the greatest tribulation mankind has ever experienced. God's wrath is to be literally poured out without mercy upon this idolatrous, Christ-rejecting society.

> "For then shall be great tribulation, such as was not since the beginning of the world to this time, no, nor ever shall be" (Matthew 24:21).

---

[1]"Enter ye in at the strait gate: for wide *is* the gate, and broad *is* the way, that leadeth to destruction, and many there be which go in thereat: Because strait *is* the gate, and narrow *is* the way, which leadeth unto life, and few there be that find it" (Matthew 7:13, 14).

For more than 6,000 years, God has pled with man to heed His warnings, but in obstinate self-will, man is determined to follow the inclinations of his own unregenerate heart, which is "deceitful above all *things*, and desperately wicked …" (Jeremiah 17:9).

> "And this is the condemnation, that light is come into the world, and men loved darkness rather than light, because their deeds were evil" (John 3:19).

Man, in his fallen state, would rather follow his own lofty, natural instincts than the lowly example of love and service exemplified in the life and teachings of Christ.

All nature obeys God; even Satan and the demons are subject to His commands (Matthew 8:27–34). But man, the crown of His creation, having been given a will of his own, chooses to go his own way. Imagining himself to be a little god with no restraints, he thinks and acts independently of His Maker, and thereby, alienates himself from the one and only source of help in the universe.

This leaves God with only one alternative: He must destroy evil men from the face of the earth if He is to salvage His creation from the wreckage, which Satan has imposed. God's desire is to bring all men to repentance and submission of His will; but when they refuse to heed His admonitions, they must suffer the consequence of His wrath, which is eternal damnation.

This is not to say that God is the author of evil. Satan gets the credit for that! His rebellion against God was the beginning of sin in the universe, and he is the undisputed originator of all negative forces. But God is still in the control tower, and where there is a whirlwind and a storm, He has command of it, makes His way through it and serves His purposes by it.

> "… the LORD hath his way in the whirlwind and in the storm … The mountains quake at him …" (Nahum 1:3, 5).

> "He looketh on the earth, and it trembleth: he toucheth the hills, and they smoke" (Psalm 104:32).

> "… his judgments *are* in all the earth" (Psalm 105:7).

In a very real sense, Satan is the cause of all evil in the universe. Without him there would be no evil, but God is always on the scene, exercising His sovereignty over both good and evil, harnessing and loosing, restraining and releasing as He sees fit.

God, who is all goodness and righteousness, can only produce after His kind. He can not and will not be the originator of anything that is harmful and destructive. However, since evil can only be destroyed with evil, He permits the releasing of Satanic power and uses it to accomplish His own eternal purposes, which will involve the final annihilation of all who oppose Him.

When John the Baptist came heralding the coming of the Messiah, he proclaimed, "And now also the axe is laid unto the root of the trees: therefore every tree which bringeth not forth good fruit is hewn down, and cast into the fire" (Matthew 3:10).

God harnesses and uses Satan's destructive devices to fight evil, much like you and I would use a sharp axe to cut down obnoxious plants that are invading our property. It is Satan divided against himself that will finally bring him and all of his followers down to hell and reduce them to ashes (Mark 3:23–27; Isaiah 14:12–14; Ezekiel 28:18).

God is a God of love and mercy and longsuffering, "not willing that any should perish, but that all should come to repentance" (2 Peter 3:9). Although He is sovereign over His own creation, and is at liberty to do what He wills with His own, He is also a God of righteousness; therefore, He never acts in judgment without first sending out warnings to those in peril.

Through Noah, a preacher of righteousness, God warned the people for a space of 120 years before sending the flood-waters of destruction upon them. Every blow of the hammer upon the ark was a call to repentance toward God, but to no avail.

Jonah was sent to prophesy the overthrow of Nineveh, and to his surprise, the people repented in sackcloth and ashes, and God spared the city for several generations. But 150 years later, they returned to their old, sinful practices, even becoming more corrupt than before, and the Lord sent the prophet Nahum to **spell their doom**. Their sentence was now irrevocable. It fell hard upon them **without mercy**.

Numerous prophets were sent to Israel in the days of her declension and apostasy to warn of the consequences of her idolatry and waywardness. God loved Israel with an undying love. He wept for her and pled with her, even predicting the Assyrian and Babylonian captivities and the worldwide dispersion of her people in punishment for her wrongdoing.

> "But they obeyed not, neither inclined their ear, but made their neck stiff, that they might not hear, nor receive instruction" (Jeremiah 17:23).

> "And they said, There is no hope: but we will walk after our own devices, and we will every one do the imagination of his evil heart" (Jeremiah 18:12).

They were given chance after chance to repent and turn back to God and survive as a **nation under God,** but they continued their disobedience and the worship of heathen gods brought the promised judgment. God's patience wore thin, and He let the axe fall. Her cities were demolished, and her people scattered, like chaff to the ends of the earth.

Modern history is replete with like warnings in the face of impending world destruction. Countless cities have been overthrown, nations conquered, regimes cast down, and whole civilizations reduced to heaps of rubble, but not without first having been given a chance to repent and survive.

Today, **world judgment** looms large on the horizon. Danger signals are flashing from shore to shore, and repentance is long overdue!

Christ could appear at any moment, bringing world history to a sudden, devastating climax!

Chapter 4
DEATH OF A WORLD

No sane person would deny that the world is in greater peril today than at any time since the **deluge**, when God sent the floodwaters of destruction upon wicked, rebellious mankind. Iniquity abounds from one end of the earth to the other. Obscenity, lasciviousness, rape, incest, harlotry and seduction are rampant. There are wars, famines, pestilences, afflictions, abominations, betrayals, and persecutions. Great astrological and terrestrial disturbances are bringing distress and perplexity to millions of people the world over.

False christs and false prophets are deceiving multitudes into following their own pernicious ways, giving heed to **seducing spirits** and **doctrines of devils** (2 Peter 2:1, 2; 1 Timothy 4:1).

Many Christians are wondering why this chaotic condition exists today. They wonder when "earth peace" will come as promised in Luke 2:14. They forget that it is first "Glory to God in the highest." Then, and only then, will there be peace on earth.

Was it Christ's purpose at His first coming to establish peace on earth? Let the Word of God speak for itself,

> "Think not that I am come to send peace on earth: I came not to send peace, but a sword" (Matthew 10:34).

> "Suppose ye that I am come to give peace on earth? I tell you, Nay; but rather division: For from henceforth there shall be five in one house divided, three against two, and two against three" (Luke 12:51, 52).

> "And a man's foes *shall be* they of his own household" (Matthew 10:36).

Here was Jesus' prediction concerning the impact of His presence and message during this age of grace. There would be division over His teachings: acceptance and rejection, adherence and digression, misconception, misinterpretation, and misapplication. This would lead to disagreement, disruption, contention, and confusion, rather than peace and harmony.

The Word of God is strangely divisive. Acting as a wedge, it separates the believer from the unbeliever, the spiritual from the unspiritual, the holy from the unholy, the good from the bad. Herein lies the principle source of disagreement among men the world over. Herein is the underlying cause of division, which will bring about the inevitable destruction of the last world kingdoms.

Without lifting a hand in defiance of His oppressors, the mere presence and utterance of Christ gave rise to a state of contention among men which is destined to end in the tearing down, breaking to pieces, and grinding to powder of the whole world structure which man has built upon the shifting sands of human knowledge and manipulation.

Not one time during Christ's ministry on earth did He say that the world would be converted during this age. Not once did He say that a reign of peace and righteousness would engulf the earth during His absence. On the contrary, He did teach that the Gospel message would, in great measure, be rejected, and that the age would end in a dreadful, sweeping apostasy.

This truth is clearly brought out in Jesus' parables recorded in Matthew 13, which describe the end results of the preaching of the Gospel to a skeptical, unbelieving world. Instead of a great, worldwide revival of faith and repentance, we see a picture of a **partly converted Church** in an **unconverted world**.

Even within the kingdom itself, which represents all of Christendom (the body of professed believers), we see both wheat (children of God) and tares (children of the wicked one) growing in the same field right down to the end of the age (vs. 24–30). We see both good and bad fish being swooped up into the great ecumenical net (vs. 31, 32), and the whole conglomerate mass being permeated with the leaven[1] of false doctrine (v. 33).

Yet, the genuine and the counterfeit bear such close similarity that only the angels of God can be entrusted with their separation at the time of the harvest. When Jesus' disciples suggested an immediate separation of the bad from among the good, He admonished them, "Nay; lest while ye gather up the tares, ye root up also the wheat with them. Let

---

[1]Leaven, when used in Scripture, has an evil connotation. Jesus warned against the "leaven of the Pharisees, which is hypocrisy" (Luke 12:1). The church at Corinth was commanded to purge out the old leaven of malice and wickedness and keep the feast with the unleavened bread of sincerity and truth (1 Corinthians 5:6-11). It represents a spurious growth, not genuine.

both grow together until the harvest: and in the time of harvest I will say to the reapers, Gather ye together first the tares, and bind them in bundles to burn them: but gather the wheat into my barn" (Matthew 13:29, 30).

We 20th century Christians are witnessing the binding together of the tares in preparation for burning in the great "Day of God's Wrath." The process is clearly evident in the many-faceted cults and false religious systems of our day, which are drawing people by the millions into their intricate webs of mysticism and demonology. It is also evident in our social structure, where the unsuspecting masses are drawn into bundles through purely humanistic interest and endeavors.

God's field (the world) has been invaded by the enemy (the devil) (Matthew 13:38, 39), who through deceit and intrigue, has taken over the reins of our present world order. Consequently, the bulk of the whole human race has fallen prey to "the rulers of the darkness of this world, against spiritual wickedness in high *places*" (Ephesians 6:12).

In the first century AD, the Apostle John wrote, "*And* we know that we are of God, and the whole world lieth in wickedness" (1 John 5:19). If this was true in the first century, how much more in this day of declension and apostasy!

God's purpose is not to save this present world-system, nor to improve our degenerating, ailing social order, but to rescue men from the powers of darkness to which they have fallen prey (Colossians 1:13), and to prepare them for a place in eternity with Christ in His coming kingdom of glory.

It is an indisputable fact that the presence of God's people in the world has had a definite, positive influence upon certain segments of our society. However, when we view the entire picture, we are forced to admit that the "tares" have multiplied at a far greater pace than the "wheat" and their obnoxious hordes[2] have filled the earth with wickedness and violence.

A satanic conspiracy undermines our entire social structure, and God's only remedy is to bring it to completion. The whole world-system, as we know it today, is soon to crumble into the dust of human error upon which it is built.

Our world is on the demise. Having rejected God's one way to salvation (Christ), it is now in the throes of death and disintegration as it moves swiftly toward Armageddon and the "Great White Throne Judgment." Having failed to bring forth fruit unto righteousness, our present world-system is soon to be hewn down and cast into the fire of God's wrath (Isaiah 12:9–11; Revelation 6:17).

The world[3] is anti-God, anti-Christ and anti-Christian (John 15:18, 19). It hates the very name of Jesus (John 7:7), spurns His counsel (Luke 7:30) and crucifies Him afresh each day with its ungodly words and deeds (Jude 15). Consequently, it is under the condemnation and judgment of God (John 3:18, 19).

---

[2]Today, there are five billion people in the world with approximately seventy-five percent without Christ.

[3] "World" (Gr. Kosmos): refers to the order, "arrangements" under which Satan has organized the world of unbelieving mankind upon his cosmic principles of force, greed, selfishness, ambition and pleasure (Matt. 4:8, 9; John 12:31, 14:30, 18:36; Eph. 6:12; 1 John 2:15–17).

"This world system is imposing and powerful with armies and fleets; is often outwardly religious, scientific, cultured, and elegant; but, seething with national and commercial rivalries and ambitions, is upheld in any real crisis only by armed force, and is dominated by satanic principles" (Scofield Reference Bible).

Chapter 5
LAST DAYS

The Holy Spirit revealed the wickedness of the last days unto the Apostle Paul as follows:

> "… in the last days perilous times shall come. For men shall be lovers of their own selves, covetous, boasters, proud, blasphemers, disobedient to parents, unthankful, unholy, Without natural affection, trucebreakers, false accusers, incontinent, fierce, despisers of those that are good, Traitors, heady, highminded, lovers of pleasures more than lovers of God; Having a form of godliness, but denying the power thereof: from such turn away … Ever learning, and never able to come to the knowledge of the truth" (2 Timothy 3:1–5, 7).

Does this look like a converted world? Is this the type of material with which one might hope to establish a righteous and peaceful world order? The thought is preposterous. Yet, that is exactly what has been attempted during the last century. Our religious and political leaders, many of them God's own children, have earnestly and persistently attempted to bring about an ideal state of affairs throughout the world based on the equality and great **brotherhood of man**.

Following World War I, a concentrated effort was made

to reform the world and establish lasting peace terms through committees, leagues, trade treaties, good-will tours, and the promotion of extensive social and religious programs.

We began to beat our swords into plowshares and to cry "Peace, peace; when *there is* no peace" (Jeremiah 6:14). Concessions were made, treaties were signed, leagues were formed and the great kingdom program was launched. The church joined hands with community welfare workers and all went forth with concerted effort to preserve the peace and make the world a better place in which to live.

Then, when all such efforts failed and this woebegone planet was cast into the throes of a second World War, we again unsheathed the sword and set out to check and subdue the evil forces. Many were led to believe that this second world conflict would be the last war, the war to end all wars, and that out of it would emerge the great peace.

To this end, the great news of bringing in **the kingdom of God** was lauded from pulpits around the world, and the churches, supposing it to be their religious duty to "bring it in," became the most staunch supporters of the war effort. Mobilizing under the blasphemous refrain, "Praise the Lord and pass the ammunition," we again squelched the enemy, this time stooping to mass slaughter through the use of atomic warfare.

Sallying forth from this bloody massacre with jubilant hearts and dripping fingers, we salved our corporate conscience and launched out upon the greatest effort of all time to preserve the peace. A United Nations organization, where nations could resolve their differences before coming to blows with one another, appeared to be a perfect solution to the international dilemma.

A noble effort, indeed! But time has proven it to be little more.

> "We looked for peace, but no good *came; and* for a time of health, and behold trouble!" (Jeremiah 8:15).

Even a casual glance at the intervening years tells the sad story of "wars and rumours of wars ... nation shall rise against nation, and kingdom against kingdom" (Matthew 24:6, 7).

Since the drawing up of the United Nations charter and the opening of the First Assembly, the Chinese and Soviet communists have pushed and fought and gobbled up their neighbors and surrounding territories until a third of the world's peoples have been sucked into their giant anti-God political and military machines.

Our own country has actively participated in a three-year Korean War and a twelve-year undeclared war in Vietnam, and most of the smaller nations have been embroiled in war at one time or another. The Middle East is a caldron of hatred, jealousy and strife.

At present, the whole world is armed to the teeth with nuclear stockpiles continually mounting, and in spite of all the *détente* and shuttling back and forth of peace agents, the threat of a third world war is an impending reality.

This all adds up to one indisputable fact: War to end all war is an elusive pipe dream. The only war to end all wars will be the war declared by God. The United Nations will not be calling the shots. There will be no bargaining with other countries. There will be no alliances to determine sides. It will be the forces of Satan against the God of glory. Do not forget that,

"The LORD *is* a man of war: the LORD *is* his name" (Exodus 15:3).

"He maketh wars to cease unto the end of the earth; he breaketh the bow, and cutteth the spear in sunder; he burneth the chariot in the fire" (Psalm 46:9).

When God declares war on Satan, we will then see the war to end all wars (Revelation 20:7–10)! Until then, we are wasting our time trying to bring in the kingdom without the King!

Looking back over the centuries of time, this troubled old earth has never known twelve consecutive months of peace. Somewhere, sword has clashed against sword and spear against spear in every month of the Christian era. Great guns have belched their tons of steel, bringing death to thousands upon thousands, and huge bombs have made rubble of habitation and habitant alike. The restless sea has received countless dead from the embattled navies of the world, and men have murdered and slain in every corner of this blood-drenched planet.

The whole inhabited earth reeks with misery, want, woe, disappointment, heartache, jealousy, hatred and strife. The hydrogen bomb and long-range missile hang like a death pall over every country of the globe, striking fear into the hearts of all mankind, and a skeptical, unbelieving world looks on in doubt and cynicism concerning God's promise of "peace on earth, good will toward men," as proclaimed by the angels at the time of Jesus' birth.

Such skepticism comes from ignorance of the Scriptures. For although God's ultimate purpose is to establish peace on earth, Christ, through necessity, came first to divide Satan's forces and to set them at variance with one another so that He might spoil principalities and powers (Colossians 2:15), and "destroy him that had the power of death, that is, the devil" (Hebrews 2:14).

So then, Christ's first advent had a two-fold purpose: to call out from among the Gentiles "a people for his name" (Acts 15:14), and to set in motion a chain of events, which is destined to culminate in the total and final destruction of Satan's evil forces, in order to make way for the coming world kingdom of peace and righteousness.

There can be no reign of peace on earth so long as Satan is running at large and sin and death are reigning. Even the Lord Himself could not produce such a condition until he, the enemy of all righteousness, is put in bondage and his power destroyed forever.

> "Or else how can one enter into a strong man's house, and spoil his goods, except he first bind the strong man? and then he will spoil his house" (Matthew 12:29).

Man has not the power to bind the strong man (Satan), neither to spoil his goods, though he is foolish enough to attempt it. This passage will be literally fulfilled at the return of Christ in glory, at which time Satan will be bound and cast into the bottomless pit for 1,000 years (Revelation 20:1–3).

Then, and only then, can there be any lasting peace on earth. Then "… shall the God of heaven set up a kingdom, which shall never be destroyed …" (Daniel 2:44).

> "Of the increase of *his* government and peace *there shall be* no end ... The zeal of the LORD of hosts [not the zeal of man] will perform this" (Isaiah 9:7).

Man's blind faith in his ability to subdue the satanic forces, and his unreasonable, optimistic hope of converting the world and establishing lasting peace terms before the return of Christ, have no biblical foundation. A spiritual reign of righteousness that does not project itself into the physical realm of humanity is without efficacy. The thought of an earthly kingdom without the personal, reigning King is the height of absurdity.

God's children are, and rightly should be, lovers of peace and order. But it is mere wishful thinking on our part to believe that we can salvage this evil world, either by regeneration or Christian education, prior to the return of Christ in glory. God never gave us such a stupendous task, and no manner of work or wishful thinking on our part could bring such a desire to fruition.

The church's commission is to evangelize the world—to get the Gospel message out to all nations, so that every individual is given a chance to accept or reject the saving grace of our Lord Jesus Christ—then leave the outcome in the hands of God.

At the appointed time Jesus will return to claim His rightful inheritance, and to redeem His creation from under the curse which Satan has imposed. Then Satan's head will be bruised and his voice forever silenced.

Chapter 6
BRINGING IN THE KINGDOM

The much used term "bringing in the kingdom," has no scriptural basis. It is an outgrowth of the union of Church and State under Constantine, and had its beginning in the fourth century.

When Constantine became emperor of the Roman Empire in AD 323, the "Church" of Rome was highly organized, almost to the point of being a monarchy under the complete control of power-wielding bishops.

Seeing the advantage he might gain from the support of such a militant group, Constantine professed faith in the Christian religion and sought to raise "Christianity" to an equal footing with paganism. Although professing to be a "Christian," he was treacherous and cruel, and remained more pagan than "Christian." Yet, he had great dreams of expanding his empire and sought to move heaven and earth to achieve his purpose.

By stretching biblical truth to suit his own fancy, Constantine concocted the idea that through a unification of the influential church group and the empirical Roman government,[1] he could usher in the millennial reign of peace

---

[1]In AD 476, when the western branch of the Roman Empire fell, the Bishop of Rome (later designated Pope) took the throne of the deposed Emperor Augustus and has retained it to this day.

and righteousness without the return of Christ, who is destined to be its King.

Since some Scripture was needed to promote such a program, Constantine claimed that the Jews had been cast off forever and that all of the promises relating to Israel's future glory were intended for the church. Consequently, under his influence and direction, the "church" became rich and powerful and deviated from its path of separation and servanthood.

Needless to say, Constantine's dreams were never realized. However, these incidents gave a rise to the postmillennial theory[2], which has prevailed throughout the centuries, as evidenced by Pope John Paul's journeying up and down the breath of the land with his compassionate cry of "Peace, peace; when *there is* no peace" (Jeremiah 6:14). If he would only tell them that **Jesus is coming soon** to make all things right, He could bring both peace and hope to their troubled hearts. He is healing "the hurt *of the daughter* of my people slightly ..." (Jeremiah 6:14), by implanting in their hearts a longing for world peace, yet deceiving them into believing it can be attained without the presence of the Prince of Peace in their midst.

There is one major error in this kind of reasoning. Man is neither good enough nor wise enough to cope with Satan and his forces.

---

[2]The main thrust of this theory is that man, in the strength of his own good-will and wisdom, will one day succeed in turning this wicked old world around, making it a veritable paradise. Then, when everything is in order, Jesus will return to take up His scepter and rule over all.

> "For we wrestle not against flesh and blood, but against principalities, against powers, against the rulers of the darkness of this world, against spiritual wickedness in high *places*" (Ephesians 6:12).

If we could for one moment, look into the spiritual realm of existence and see the battles raging between God's holy angels and Satan's forces, we would be frightened out of our wits and be willing to turn it all over to the Creator and Sustainer of the universe. (See Daniel 10:12–21 and Revelation 12:7–10 for examples of this warfare.)

The postmillennial theory not only holds out false hopes to lost mankind, it relegates the event of Christ's return to earth into the distant future, and thus renders it useless and of no effect. It is a gross misinterpretation of Scripture, and has led to more religious confusion, and done more to hinder the progress and destroy the spirituality of the church, than all other doctrines combined.

Satan's one passionate desire is to alienate the affections of mankind; and the belief in a soon-returning Saviour is the one thing he cannot tolerate. Thus, he adroitly gives the lie to God's Word concerning the second coming of Christ by holding out to man the elusive hope of converting the world and setting up a system of government, which would ensure a never-ending, peaceful and prosperous existence on earth.

Such slogans as "Ushering in the Kingdom of God," "Winning the World to Christ," and "Save America to Save the World," constitute the biggest and best bait that Satan has yet cast out to the perishing multitudes who rush to take part in anything that appears to be of a religious nature, thinking to save themselves from the swift current of the undertow. It is blinding most people to the truth and leading them down blind alleys, in spite of the fact that neither Bible prophecy nor world history has ever verified its claims.

The truth of the matter is that Satan is attempting to build a world kingdom for himself through fallen mankind whom he deludes into carrying out his plans and purposes by labeling it the "kingdom of God," and thus making it appear that he is carrying out a divine plan.

To learn that the kingdoms of this world are subject to satanic control, we have only to go to the scene of Christ's temptation in the wilderness. "And the devil, taking him up into an high mountain, shewed unto him all the kingdoms of the world in a moment of time. And the devil said unto him, All this power will I give thee, and the glory of them: for that is delivered unto me; and to whomsoever I will I give it. If thou therefore wilt worship me, all shall be thine" (Luke 4:5–7).

Christ did not question Satan's claim of authority over earthly kingdoms. Neither did He meet the challenge and wrest them from the hand of the tempter as He could have done had He yielded to the subtle temptation, but He only answered,

> "... Get thee behind me, Satan: for it is written, Thou shalt worship the Lord thy God, and him only shalt thou serve" (Luke 4:8).

Jesus' statement to Pilate just before the crucifixion gives further evidence to the fact that His kingdom is not to be set up under the present dispensation. He answered,

> "... My kingdom is not of this world [world-system]: if my kingdom were of this world, then would my

> servants [the angels] fight, that I should not be delivered to the Jews: but now is my kingdom not from hence" (John 18:36).

The kingdoms of this world are humanistic at best and susceptible to satanic influence and control. They are base, changeable, at variance with one another, and subject to decadence and destruction. The past and present crumbling of all world governments is positive proof of their worldly, vacillating nature. They began to decay the very moment they began to take form. It will ever be so with human institutions.

Chapter 7
AMERICA: AN EXAMPLE

As a case in point, let us take a quick inventory of our own beloved nation, which started out with such high hopes and aspirations to be a truly Christian republic. Without equivocation and without hypocrisy, let us open the doors of our many cloistered habitations, pull out the skeletons, and take a candid view of our present stance using God's word as a measuring rod.

We adult Americans know God's laws. They are part of our Christian heritage. We cannot hide behind the cloak of ignorance when it comes to the precepts of God. So, let us take an honest, straightforward look at the situation we find ourselves in and accept our part of the blame for the hodge-podge, which we still like to think of as a form of Christian democracy.

We have the Ten Commandments before us:

1. Thou shalt have no other gods before me.
2. Thou shalt not make unto thee any graven image.
3. Thou shalt not take the name of the Lord thy God in vain.
4. Remember the sabbath day to keep it holy.
5. Honour thy father and thy mother.
6. Thou shalt not kill.
7. Thou shalt not commit adultery.

8. Thou shalt not steal.
9. Thou shalt not bear false witness against thy neighbour.
10. Thou shalt not covet.

Now, let us lay alongside them a listing of present-day, American standards as exemplified by our ultra-permissive society and judicial system of government:

1. Thou shalt worship the gods of thine own choosing. Whether they be people, possessions, money, sports, sex, entertainment or what-have-you. This is strictly your business.
2. Thou shalt not bow down to any man-made image. This is taboo in our sophisticated, enlightened age. Why turn to dead idols when you can bring any number of those "beautiful people" into your private sanctuary with the touch of a button. The field is wide open and you are free to worship them according to the dictates of your own conscience.
3. Thou shalt not take the name of the Lord God in vain, except when used on stage or screen for the relaxation and enjoyment of millions of viewers. Celebrities and other television personalities are in a class by themselves and cannot be censured for what they say or do.
4. Remember the sabbath day to keep it as you please—for pleasure, work, church attendance or the worship of your favorite gods. It is **your day**, treat it accordingly.
5. Honor thy father and thy mother, as long as they do not interfere with your private life. In that case, treat

them as you would any other person who might get in your way. Since they have **done nothing for you**, why feel responsible for their well-being or support?

6. Do not kill anyone, unless it be by abortion or euthanasia. These are permissible if agreed upon by both parties. And don't let your conscience bother you; it is only a person.
7. Do not commit adultery, except by consent of both parties. Adultery is now the accepted way of life, according to our patterns of morality. Why restrain yourself in the matter of sex? Satan gloats over your clandestine affairs, and only **you** will have to bear the consequences.
8. Thou shalt not steal, unless it could bring a sizeable booty. A good, healthy bank fraud is permissible if you can get away with it, or a secret deal with some government agency such as the Pentagon, or perhaps some large corporation where the shortage would not be easily detected. Then, when you are caught, delay your punishment through entangling court proceedings. The taxpayer will be happy to finance the prosecution.
9. Thou shalt not bear false witness against thy neighbor, unless by putting him down you can promote your own interests and those of your family. Satan is the father of lies and will be delighted with your fabrications, his tools in all wicked situations.
10. Thou shalt not covet too much of this world's goods—just enough to keep up with your rich associates. It is only human to desire what others possess in such abundance. After all, you are due your part of God's

bounty. So go ahead and envy the wealth of others, and someday maybe you will acquire a small fortune without working for it. Then when death strikes, you can leave it all behind.

Are these exaggerations? We think not. An honest appraisal of our nation's moral standards today reveals little affinity to God's commandments, and only a slight resemblance to those drawn up by our Pilgrim forefathers.

Although our founding fathers attempted to set up "one nation under God," by building Old Testament precepts into our Constitution, we perceive that deterioration and moral degradation have set in as we gradually succumbed to human frailties.

Big-hearted, patriotic, liberty-loving America, with arms stretched upward to God and outward to the world, started out with such great promise, sensing our special mission to humanity. We had truly meant to be good! Our love for God and our respect for His Word were woven into the warp and woof of our very existence. They were written into our Constitution, engraved upon our coins and emblazoned across the wide expanse of our homeland, as countless church spires and praying congregations began to dot the hills and dales of every settlement.

Yes, we had meant to be good, to worship and serve the great God of the universe who had delivered us from the tyranny of religious and political despots and blessed us far beyond anything we had ever deserved or even dreamed.

But, somewhere, somehow, things went awry. **The Enemy** had crept in and sowed tares in our field. The fortune-seekers, slave traders, conspirators, grafters, cultists, drunkards, murderers, adulterers, and prostitutes had set up camp alongside our Pilgrim and Puritan forefathers, for they, too, loved freedom—freedom to follow the dictates of their own depraved minds and hearts.

As if this was not sufficient to bring us to ruin, **our Adversary** began to bring into our midst a host of strange idols to test our mettle. One by one, he stealthily unveiled them as we stood afar off, beholding their glory! There were the gods of wealth and materialism, of power, fame and social status. Next came the gods of philosophy, higher education, our industrial might, scientific know-how and worldly wisdom. On and on they went, too numerous to mention.

Then suddenly, as if by magic, there appeared before our astonished gaze, a procession of goddesses, high and lifted up, in bold relief! There was the goddess of pleasure, of sensualism and free love, of creature comforts, entertainments and titillating amusements! There they stood in gorgeous array! So lovely to behold! And ours for the taking!

Already caught up in the enchantment of our prized possessions and outstanding accomplishments, we became easy prey to the wiles of this **cunning Tempter**. He was downright glamorous as he waved his jeweled hand over our fertile fields and expanding industries in appraisal of our fantastic wealth and progress, all the while poking fun at our pious, puritanical ideas and ideals. Beckoning us on with a swift panorama of our glorious holdings, he challenged our people to a life of pride, ease, self-indulgence, and independence of God, our Creator and Sustainer. His tactics were so subtle, his manner so gentle, we were caught up in a trance as we followed him blindly, wholly unaware of the direction in which we were going.

Little by little, generation after generation, he led us down a labyrinth of intricate tunnels and passageways until we became helplessly and hopelessly entangled in a net of our own choosing, woven thread by thread, pattern by pattern, and piece by piece, as we followed our self-propelled, self-centered pursuits.

Slowly and deftly, Satan has supplanted our one true God with false gods of our own choosing. While holding out the elusive dream of "liberty and justice for all," he has led us into a trap from which there is no escape. America's gods are legion! We worship at the shrine of **humanism**. Entertainment, sports, sex, drugs,[1] creature comforts and gross materialism are the order of the day.

We have changed the glory of the incorruptible God into an image made like unto corruptible man. Although we know God, we glorify Him not as God, neither are thankful, but have become vain in our imaginations and our foolish hearts are darkened (Romans 1:21–23).

America has been the recipient of the most bountiful supply of God's grace, has enjoyed more religious and personal freedom, and has been exposed to more gospel preaching than any other nation on the face of the earth. But we have both spurned His counsel and squandered our freedoms. We have supplanted His marvelous grace with our own volition and ingenuity.

Rejecting the True Light exposes any nation to "seducing spirits, and doctrines of devils" (1 Timothy 4:1), and the

---

[1]Dope was thrust into our country like a great tidal wave during and following the Vietnam War, a Communist move to weaken our military and bring us to the point of self-destruction. Today, the drug traffic in America is a national scandal, which threatens our very existence.

overall result is an inexorable maze of -isms and practices which lead down blind alleys to death and decay. Darkness covers our land today because we have continued to make the wrong choices, and we choose to dwell in darkness because it serves as a false covering for our sinful, rebellious ways.

Like Israel of old, we have forsaken God, the Fountain of Living Waters, and have hewn out for ourselves cisterns—"broken cisterns, that can hold no water" (Jeremiah 2:13).

Now, having passed our 200th anniversary as a so-called Christian nation, we suddenly become aware that we, too, have been susceptible to the same greed, vice and immorality which have been the undoing of every nation that has fallen before us.

Let us not be deceived.

> "... God is not mocked: for whatsoever a man soweth, that shall he also reap. For he that soweth to his flesh shall of the flesh reap corruption; but he that soweth to the Spirit shall of the Spirit reap life everlasting" (Galatians 6:7, 8).

America has sown the wind and is due to **reap a whirlwind**! Her final destiny is written in the oracles of God:

> "The wicked shall be turned into hell, *and* all the nations that forget God" (Psalm 9:17).

Nothing short of **wholesale national repentance** can delay our impending judgment!

Chapter 8
THE CULPRIT

In order to get the full import of the satanic takeover of the world, God's rightful domain, we must look back into the dateless ages of eternity past, when Satan was not the wily "old serpent" that he now is, but God's anointed cherub, with superior rank and title.

Satan is a mysterious creature, who beggars description in human terms. Although most of his past lies buried in the archives of antiquity, a thorough search of the Scriptures yields a wealth of information concerning his origin, nature and present-day antics. A rundown of his original status and eternal destiny can be found in Isaiah 14:12–17 and Ezekiel 28:1–19, where God addresses him as the prince of Tyrus (the unseen power behind the throne).

First known as Lucifer, son of the morning (Isaiah 14:12), he was the wisest, most beautiful and most powerful of all of God's original created beings. A trusted attendant at the throne of God, he was perfect in all his ways from the day he was created and basked in the light of God's favor and freedom.

It appears that God lavished all of His creative prowess upon this magnificent creature. Lucifer's body was overlaid with gold and with every kind of precious stone which shimmered and shone in the light of God's favor and firmament, as he darted about the throne of God, and from planet to planet, in the performance of his many duties.

Musical flutes were deftly built into his marvelous body, so that he made melody wherever he went (Ezekiel 28:13).

Possessing a spiritual body, he was not confined to visible form and was able to function throughout the universe. As God's anointed cherub, he was elevated to a high position and entrusted with extensive authority over some part of God's vast creation, with myriads of angels and other beings under his control.

There is abundant evidence that Lucifer's lordship extended over the original prehistoric earth, which was no doubt fully developed under his power and supervision.

Endowed with superior knowledge and beautiful to behold, this majestic creature faithfully discharged his royal duties as long as he stayed under God's controlling hand. However, his supernatural endowments were too much for his ego and proved to be his undoing (Ezekiel 28:5). He became puffed up with pride and ambition and presumptuously aspired to set his throne above the stars of God and said, "I will be like the most High" (Isaiah 14:9–23). Inducing a host of angels to join him in a rebellion against his Creator, he staged a rebellion against God's holy angels but was overthrown and cast out of God's heaven into the regions below (Luke 10:18).

The consequences of Lucifer's fall were far-reaching. God's beautiful creation was now infested with battalions of marauding rebels who were intent on thwarting His every purpose. The spiritual warfare between the forces of good and evil had now begun, and only God knew the scope of its devastation for millenniums to come.

Furthermore, everything that Lucifer had touched was contaminated, and this involved Planet Earth with all of its creatures. They, too, were corrupted by the virus of rebellion and must come under the judgment of a holy and just God. Genesis 1:2 describes the wreckage that followed: "And the earth was without form, and void; and darkness *was* upon the face of the deep."

A casual reading of Genesis 1:1–27 without other related Scripture, has led many to believe that God began the creation of our solar system by carelessly flinging a blob of unrelated elements into space and then taking millions of years to prepare it for human habitation. This is not true! God, being a perfect God, could not and would not have produced a planet so utterly void of shape and usefulness as we encounter in Genesis 1:2. Here we have a picture of utter **chaos** in the midst of **divine order**, which is not at all commensurate with the panorama of creation and could only be the result of God's judgment upon wicked and rebellious subjects.

Between Genesis 1:1 and Genesis 1:2, **something happened**. We find the earth without form in verse 2, and yet Isaiah 45:18 says,

> "For thus saith the LORD that created the heavens; God himself that formed the earth and made it; he hath established it, he created it not in vain, he formed it to be inhabited: I *am* the LORD; and *there is* none else."

So, in actuality, we are reading in Genesis 1 about a "re-creation" after the judgment of God on His original creation; all due to the rebellious cherub called Lucifer. Further proof for this is seen in Genesis 1:28 where God tells Adam and Eve to **replenish** the earth, clearly implying it had been plenished before.

We are not suggesting there were other men on the earth before Adam, for he is the first man (1 Corinthians 15:45–47). We do, however, accept the scriptural fact that there was a flood before Noah's flood (study carefully 2 Peter 3:5–7), and there were other "beings" before human beings on the earth! It would be incongruous to presume that the Omnipotent God, who set the boundless universe with all its galaxies in perfect array,[1] and holds all in place by the **word of His power** (Hebrews 1:3), would resort to such crude methods as though He were a man and not God.

Psalm 33:6, 9 tells us the exact manner in which the entire universe came into existence: "By the word of the LORD were the heavens made;[2] and all the host of them by the breath of his mouth … For he spake, and it was *done*; he commanded, and it stood fast." This is reiterated in Psalm 148:5, and again in Isaiah 48:3, where God vehemently proclaims that all things from the beginning "went forth out of my mouth … I did *them* suddenly, and they came to pass."

The Bible opens with the sublime statement, "In the beginning God created the heaven and the earth" (Genesis 1:1). What God is telling us here is that our planet and its surrounding heaven were a part of His original creation in the dateless ages of past eternity. This would have included the entire universe with all of its myriads of galaxies, and it could

---

[1]Some twentieth century astronomers have estimated that 100 million galaxies exist within a billion light years from the earth. Some of these galaxies contain millions of stars, or suns. Our nearest star is said to be 25 trillion miles from the earth. These figures give some idea of the vastness of God's Creation.

[2]The Scriptures distinguish three heavens: first, the lower heaven, or region of the clouds; second, the second or planetary heavens; and third, the heaven of heavens, the abode of God (Scofield Bible Note).

even mean that the earth was God's first creative venture. If so, this would explain His consuming interest in, and undying love for, the earth and its fallen creatures.

Whatever is meant, all was spoken into existence, "In the beginning," and all was perfect in the minutest detail. No doubt, the original earth was beautiful beyond imagination, with a super-abundant growth of vegetation and enormous creatures, which would make our present earth look dwarfed in comparison.

But at some point in God's program things went awry, and the earth was cast into the throes of death and destruction. There can be only one explanation. This once beautiful planet had come under the **judgment** of the **Creator**. The entire scene had been wrecked by some violent force and lay in total ruin[3]—a formless mass buried beneath a crust of ice and thick darkness (Genesis 1:2). Lucifer's domain—the original, primeval earth—had been demolished by violent convulsions of land and sea, entombing all living things within its icy grave, and hiding the light of the heavenly bodies in the darkness of a murky atmosphere.

Everywhere there are visible signs of just such a cataclysmic upheaval of the earth's surface as described here. Our hills and valleys, mountains and ocean craters, the fissures, faults and fossils, the coal and rock formations, and mineral deposits—all are conclusive evidence of the violent convulsions that brought ruin to a world civilization, which existed in the pre-dawn of man's history.

---

[3]Isaiah 14:17 tells us that Lucifer (Satan) made the world a wilderness and destroyed the cities thereof, inferring that God permitted him to destroy the works of His own hands, perhaps by a chain reaction accidentally set off as he experimented with splitting the atom.

There is no indication of the time element involved in God's initial creative acts and the judgment that followed Satan's rebellion. Millions of years could have elapsed between the first act of creation (Genesis 1:1) and the moving of God's Spirit upon the waters to bring restoration.

The millions of years which science demands for the formation of the earth, its buried fossils, and the Carboniferous and Ice Ages, all are given a wide margin in the opening verses of the Genesis record. All prehistoric animal life and the earth's proliferous vegetation would have been buried under the molten rock and soil by the violent convulsions that occurred.

No doubt, eons of time were involved in the original creation and duration of this primeval order, giving room for all of the geological ages, which scientific discoveries claim for the existence of prehistoric inhabitants of our planet, and shutting the mouths of godless evolutionists.

The **re-establishment** of the earth as described in Genesis 1:3–24 is merely a continuation of God's plan to create and to impart life. It is an account of the restoration of the earth to productivity—the calling forth of heavenly bodies already created, the germination of plant seeds, which were lying dormant beneath the earth's surface, and the creation of man and beast to **RE**-plenish (fill up again) and dominate it.[4]

---

[4]Many theologians reject this interpretation of the Scriptures, but until we acknowledge the fact of a fully developed, inhabited pre-Adamite earth, and envision Genesis 1:2 as the result of Divine judgment, the battle between science and the Genesis record of creation will go on, and multitudes will continue to be deceived thereby.

Chapter 9
SATAN CAST OUT

Satan's rebellion was the beginning of sin in the universe and opened up a perpetual warfare between the forces of good and evil that has been raging in the heavenlies, as well as on earth, for over 6,000 years.

In return for his rebellion, he and all his cohorts were cast out of God's heaven to the regions below (Luke 10:18), but this did not daunt his rebellious spirit. It only served to intensify his diabolical schemes to usurp the sovereignty of God. Capitalizing on his supernal attributes, he set up a base of operation somewhere in the outer realms of our galaxy and from there continued his relentless maneuvers. With the restoration of the earth and the reappearance of light, Satan's attention was at once attracted, and he came back seeking control once more of his lost domain.

Then, when man was created, he became the perfect target for Satan's assaults. Adam, made in the image of God with a free will of his own, had been delegated the responsibility of replenishing and dominating the earth. Obviously, whoever controlled his mind and heart would control both man and his domain.

Here was Satan's chance! He had only to break down man's allegiance to his Creator. Then, he could claim all for his own and disrupt God's plan for both man and Planet

Earth. This he did in the Garden of Eden. Sending his evil spirit into the serpent, he tempted Adam and Eve by disrupting God's word and holding out inducements for disobedience. In exchange for life, he offered them **knowledge**. They took it and plunged themselves and all their posterity into the abyss of spiritual death (Genesis 3:5–7).

Furthermore, having made the wrong choice, they would have to suffer the physical consequences of their decision. The earth, under the curse, would henceforth bring forth "thorns" and "thistles" against which man must battle for his very existence, until he at last would succumb to the dust from which he was formed (Genesis 3:17–19). Thus, sin found lodgement in the heart of man, and his soul became subject to Satan's power and influence and the battleground between the forces of good and evil.

Man had been given dominion over the earth, and when he fell into the hands of Satan, the earth and everything in it fell victim to Satan's power. From that day to this, his every effort has been bent on building up and increasing that power in the vain hope of repossessing it for his own.

Satan's one passionate desire is to alienate the affections of mankind and, through him, to set up his own socialistic, one-world system of government, designed to endure the ravages of time and metamorphose into a **grandiose utopia**. This was in back of his sinister proposal to Christ when he offered Him all the kingdoms of the world and the glory of them if He would fall down and worship him (Matthew 4:1–11).

Today, Satan is making that same proposition to man, and his temporary success is phenomenal. Since practically all material things are at his command through unregenerate mankind, he has unlimited resources with which to work.

Through his cunning devices and the multitude of his traffic in merchandise, he supplies temporary satisfaction for the soul of man through the carnal nature and wins him over to his way of thinking and acting.

Satan's throne is somewhere in the celestial sphere, which surrounds the earth. He is the "prince of the power of the air" (Ephesians 2:2). Somewhere within the outer realms of our galaxy there is an anti-region made up of anti-matter, which he has constructed through millions of years of experimentation and probings into the secrets of nature. A serious study of the Word of God reveals a place somewhere above the second heaven called "the deep" and sometimes "the sea." (Study Genesis 1:2; Job 26:5–13; 38:7–11, 30; Psalm 148:1–7.) There must be a great body of water above our heads! Don't forget that Noah's flood was a result of "all the fountains of the great deep broken up . . ." (Genesis 7:11). Satan is called "leviathan" in Isaiah 27:1 and, according to Job 41, this leviathan resides in the deep! That is why he is in the amphibian class and is described in Job 41 as a dragon which maketh the **deep** to boil like a pot. (See also Revelation 12:9.) From this vaunted, self-appointed position, he directs his own ceaseless activities in a desperate attempt to thwart every purpose of God.

As Beelzebub, the prince of devils (Matthew 12:24), he commands a highly regimented army of principalities and powers (Ephesians 6:12), who are engineering his maniacal schemes for conquest. His fiendish goal is to bring the earth and its solar system under his own, complete control before Christ returns to take over the reins and set up His righteous world kingdom.

Satan knows the time is short and that if he fails (which he will), he is headed for the bottomless pit where he will be held at bay for a thousand years, only to be brought up later and cast into the lake of fire (Revelation 20:1–3, 10).

Fallen mankind is the medium through which Satan works. Through a gradual impartation of the secrets of the universe, he leads us on in our quest for more and more technological proficiency with which to conquer space and gain access to the regions beyond. In benevolent, high-handed fashion, we defy God's laws of gravity and ascend with him into the heavens in utter disregard for the bounds of our habitation, which God has before ordained (Psalm 115:16; Acts 17:26).

This dogmatic determination to intrude into the secrets of God's universe was Lucifer's atrocious sin for which he was consigned to the lake of fire (Isaiah 14:13–15). His inducement to man to "come up higher" is a mere continuation of his own initial venture to set his throne above the stars of God and become the supreme power of the universe.

We know not how far God permitted the wise men of the antediluvian age to go in the wicked imaginations of their hearts, but we do know that He drew an ultimatum and sent the flood-waters of destruction upon them.

Following this awful judgment, a group of presumptuous schemers set out to build a tower that would reach unto heaven (a ziggurat from which they could study the heavens and try to prognosticate the future). They said,

> "... Go to, let us build us a city and a tower, whose top *may reach* unto heaven; and let us make us a name, lest we be scattered abroad upon the face of the whole earth" (Genesis 11:4).

But God said,

> "Behold, the people *is* one, and they have all one language; and this they begin to do: and now nothing will be restrained from them, which they have imagined to do … let us go down, and there confound their language, that they may not understand one another's speech" (Genesis 11:6, 7).

And so the Lord brought about the very thing they feared and were attempting to prevent.

> "So the LORD scattered them abroad from thence upon the face of all the earth: and they left off to build the city" (Genesis 11:8).

Chapter 10
MAN'S REBELLION

Today man is saying, "Let us discover the secrets of the universe...let us use those powers for national and personal aggrandizement...to gain power over the elements and become masters of our destiny. Let us devise and invent, promote and explore, let us be one mind and together establish a universal society that will endure the ravages of time."

But God answers,

> "... I will destroy the wisdom of the wise, and will bring to nothing the understanding of the prudent" (1 Corinthians 1:19).

> "... I will shake the heavens and the earth; And I will overthrow the throne of kingdoms, and I will destroy the strength of the kingdoms ..." (Haggai 2:21, 22).

Again, God determines to bring about the very thing man fears and is foolishly trying to prevent. The reason is obvious. Man has renounced God's lordship over himself and his domain. He has lived and worked, planned and builded, organized and promoted, without taking God into his confidence.

It is one thing to acknowledge God as Creator of the universe, but quite a different matter to seek His will as revealed in Holy Writ. It is one thing to blatantly proclaim Christ as Son of God and Saviour of the world, but quite a different thing to follow the lowly pathway of service and obedience set out in His life and teachings.

Every human being is aware that he should both worship God and seek His counsel in all that he undertakes. But men have refused both worship and counsel and as a result have become "vain in their imaginations, and their foolish heart was darkened. Professing themselves to be wise, they became fools …" (Romans 1:21, 22).

As a result, God's prediction that in the last days "they shall walk like blind men" (Zephaniah 1:17) is today finding fulfillment in the blundering errors of human reasoning.

God says,

> "Woe unto *them that are* wise in their own eyes, and prudent in their own sight! … Woe to the rebellious children … that take counsel, but not of me … that they may add sin to sin" (Isaiah 5:21; 30:1).

Men devise and invent, construct and explore, predict and decree—all without asking counsel of God. Then they arrogantly cast their paltry achievements at the feet of the Almighty Creator and **implore His blessings** upon them. Everything from the hydrogen bomb to the birth control pill is dedicated to God and promoted in behalf of social advancement. We have become "inventors of evil things" (Romans 1:30). Our reckless generation knows no technological restraints.[1] What has not already been accomplished, the scientist believes that he can and will accomplish, if given the time and money.

Where do we get the idea that God is in everything man has the ability to accomplish? God is not in organized crime, nor in social injustice, nor racial prejudice, nor is He in child abuse. Yet, He permits all of these to continue and even to accelerate for centuries without checking them. Have we forgotten that there is an enemy in the camp who imparts to mankind a type of knowledge and wisdom that is diametrically opposed to God, that Satan seeks to exalt men in their own eyes and to cause them to imagine themselves to be in the will of God, when in fact, they are serving his own interests?

It is no surprise when the groping multitudes stand in worshipful adoration before man's fantastic achievements, but when the Lord's children join in the ranks of the cheering parade, we become a spectacle in ourselves. What a travesty of reasoning we must present to the unbelieving world when we become so enamored with scientific exploits that we salute each new journey into space as a sign of God's favor. What a paradox we create when we proclaim His approval of every spectacular exhibition!

When the Almighty Creator gave man domination over the earth, He issued no decree concerning his right of access to the regions beyond, and nothing short of willful arrogance could lead to the assumption that He did.

God has provided only One Way for man's entrance into the heavenlies, and that is through the atoning blood of His

---

[1]The atom is God's building block in creation. How dare we tear it apart for any reason! Man's folly is his doom!

Son, Jesus Christ, who says: "I am the door: by me if any man enter in, he shall be saved … He that entereth not by the door … but climbeth up some other way, the same is a thief and a robber" (John 10:9, 1). Thieves and robbers enter where their presence is forbidden and unwanted and will one day have to pay for their folly.

As present-day scientists fling their manned ships into space and devise plans for further explorations of distant planets in search of extraterrestrial beings, one cannot help but wonder how far they will be permitted to go in their deft accomplishments. One thing is certain: God has drawn a line, and they will not cross it!

Military might is the ultimate goal of all space exploits, as major powers vie for superiority. Plans now being projected for manned military space stations carrying killer satellites will soon be finalized, and the ruling power will come into focus.

There is no doubt but that atomic energy will be the power through which the Antichrist will rule the world as he holds all nations at bay with the threat of total annihilation. Star Wars will soon become a reality!

Scientific knowledge is not only threatening our faith and dependence on God—it is weakening our entire civilization as we are held in the grip of its domination. In rejecting God and refusing to be guided by His statutes, the great stream of humanity has fallen prey to the Tempter's wiles, seemingly oblivious to the danger ahead and in total disregard for the "One Way" of escape. Thus, Satan obtains a fatal grip on the world as multitudes follow him blindly to the very precipice of death and destruction.

Chapter 11
SATAN'S TACTICS

"Yea, hath God said, Ye shall not eat of every tree of the garden?" (Genesis 3:1).

Satan's only hope of regaining possession of his lost domain lies in his ability to get complete control of mankind, and he works feverishly night and day to accomplish this end. While posing as a do-gooder and pretending to exalt civilization to the status of the gods, he is in reality dragging us down to dishonor and degradation. His age-old query, "Yea, hath God said," has cast the whole world into the throes of darkness with no vested authority and no sure and certain standards by which to chart our course.

With every man left to steer his own ship—to build his own star—to do that which is right in his own eyes— the great bulk of the human race is left without an anchor and rendered vulnerable to all of the Tempter's wiles.

Using our institutions of higher learning, and even some of our theological seminaries, as seedbeds for his liberal, modernistic dogmas, this enemy of all righteousness questions the authenticity of God's Holy Word and misconstrues its tenets through endless philosophical and humanistic reasonings and twisted paraphrasings[1] until its true meaning is vague and unauthoritative. Posing as God's minister and projecting himself through false apostles and deceitful workers who transform themselves into the apostles of Christ (2 Corinthians 11:13), Satan is the propagator of numerous counterfeit cults and religions that only the Spirit-filled Christian can detect.

Denying the virgin birth, the blood-atonement, the bodily resurrection, and the personal return of Christ, he substitutes a counterfeit, socialistic type of religion, which deludes and engulfs multiplied thousands of confused followers. This confusion is enhanced by Satan's attack on the infallible, inerrant Word of God. We now have over 100 different translations since the printing of the AV-1611, King James Bible. All of the modern versions add and take away from Scripture, which is clearly forbidden (Deuteronomy. 4:2; Proverbs 30:6; and Revelation 22:19). Many professing Christians have accepted these modern versions without ever checking the **facts** that they attack the deity of Christ, the virgin birth, the blood atonement, the Trinity and other **major doctrines** of the Bible. Satan has deceived many with his "unholy bibles," disguised under the claims of being "easier to read," "more up to date," "non archaic," "closer to the originals,"[2] etc. Masquerading as an **angel of light** (2 Corinthians 11:14), and holding up the banner of world progress and cultural advancement, Satan dispenses his false theories and deceptive ideologies, which

---

[1]All paraphrased editions of the Bible are hybrids—of mixed origin—inaccurate and unreliable. They represent man's effort to supplant the original Word of God. Such deviation from the original text as Luke 2:5 and John 14:14 in the so-called "Living Bible" have no doubt contributed to the low moral standards and mock discipleship of our modern day.

[2]Serious students of the Word of God should see *New Age Versions,* by G.A. Riplinger, proving that the Bible of the Reformation, the AV-1611, King James Bible is the preserved Word of God (Ps. 12:6-7) in the English language and that all other versions are an attack on the pure Word of God.

appeal to the natural intellect but lead down a labyrinth of elusive pathways strewn with the carcasses of men and nations.

As **prince of the power of the air** (Ephesians 2:2), this marauding villain roams the heavens and earth in command of a large regimentation of wicked, unearthly creatures who constantly engage in combat duty with God's holy angels (Daniel 10:12, 13; Jude 9) and wield great authority over world affairs. His emissaries, the demons, are legion and capable of permeating every area of the personality and, consequently, every stratum of society that is not wholly surrendered to Christ.

With expert skill and ingenuity, he dispenses an artificial light of grandeur and vainglory, prestige and power, profit and sinful pleasure, worldly knowledge and humanistic wisdom by which he blinds the minds of men so that they are insensible to the things of the Spirit of Christ (2 Corinthians 4:4).

There is no end to the devastation wrought by this derelict and no direction one can turn without seeing his footprints. Everything of an evil, hurtful nature can be laid to his charge. Every thorn, every thistle, every heartache, and every teardrop can be attributed to his handiwork.

He stalks up and down our streets lining them with murder, rape, robbery, drunkenness, fear and debauchery. He builds his casinos, his theaters, his discotheques, his television towers, his massage parlors, exclusive night clubs, bars and houses of prostitution.

He promotes nudity, adultery, fornication,[3] homosexuality, pornography, abortion, woman's lib, dope addiction, the drug traffic, alcoholism, child abuse and rebellion against authority.

He packs our prisons, our hospitals, our mental institutions and juvenile courts. He disrupts our schools and communities with forced busing, racial issues, parental and child delinquency, and vandalism. He tears our homes to shreds with infidelity, drunkenness, child abuse and easy divorce.

Wars, pestilences, floods, droughts, famines, hurricanes, tornadoes, earthquakes—in short, all calamities and dilemmas are the result of Satan's meddling in the affairs of God and maneuvering the thoughts and actions of men.

Polluting the very air that we breathe through man's questionable scientific endeavors, he disrupts natural phenomena, plays havoc with weather conditions, and infiltrates every nook and cranny of the globe with "blood and toil and sweat and tears" until the whole world is filled with sorrow and tribulation.

Satan has many avenues through which he functions, and his ministers are legion. They sit in the high seats of industry and government and exercise authority over national and international affairs. Some are among the most highly educated and most socially prominent citizens of the world and oftentimes are the subjects of public respect and reverence. But if they have not the Spirit of Christ,

> "These are wells without water, clouds that are carried with a tempest; to whom the mist of darkness is reserved for ever. For when they speak great swelling *words* of vanity, they allure through the lusts

---

[3]Fornication and homosexuality are the specific sins that brought a rain of fire and brimstone upon Sodom and Gomorrah. Fornication is defined as "sexual relations between unmarried persons." Those who indulge in and promote the promiscuity of our present-day society are under the judgment of God.

> of the flesh, *through much* wantonness, those that were clean escaped from them who live in error. While they promise them liberty, they themselves are the servants of corruption …" (2 Peter 2:17–19).

With high-sounding phrases of loyalty to God and country, these national and international prognosticators make a great pretense of social concern and patriotism. Yet, underneath their shell of hypocrisy and sham, they blaspheme the very positions they pretend to hold in honor.

Like "whited sepulchers," these gluttonous winebibbers live off the fat of the land and squander public funds to satisfy their own lustful appetites. They are activated by Satan himself, who lifts them up to power and prominence and uses them like puppets to promote his own ends.

All this, and much, much more, God's enemy, that old serpent, which is called the Devil and Satan (Revelation 12:9), accomplishes through fallen mankind, who either consciously or unconsciously give their allegiance to him.

Chapter 12
BRAINWASHING THE POPULACE

Satan is a lascivious deceiver and down through the ages, dating from his first victory in the Garden of Eden, his every major triumph has been won through the practice of deceit. This deceit is the one method by which he sways the world to the tempo of his way of thinking and acting. Through the subtle channels of mysticism, occultism, satanism, astrology, witchcraft, and mind-expanding drugs, he enslaves his disciples the world over.

In virtual control of the air waves, Satan brainwashes the entire populace by pouring out a steady stream of vice and immorality in the privacy of our homes. Having been originally endowed with musical genius (Ezekiel 28:13), he cleverly creates the demoralizing rock jungle beat with its soul destroying lyrics and gyrations, which hypnotize our youth and act as a catalyst for sexual liberation.

Through confiscation of the press, stage, and screen, this flamboyant, marauding genius dispenses a constant avalanche of obscene, pornographic, sadistic muck, which has turned the mainstream of our populace into a sex-oriented, crime-ridden society.

Through the Devil's abominable creations in women's styles, he makes nudity and promiscuity appear to be a virtue and contends that the female body is to be exhibited and coddled like the bunnies of Playboy philosophy, for man's sensual pleasure and gratification.[1]

Brazenly sanctioning the animalistic approach to free love, Satan promotes premarital and extramarital sex and the mass murder of unborn babies under the flying banners of women's rights and population control. Setting forth his diabolical, libertine doctrines, he rolls out the red carpet for crime and licentiousness through legislation of all the social vices from "liquor by the drink" to homosexuality.

Women's Lib is one of his prime specialties by which Satan attempts to reverse God's intended order for the role of the sexes and disrupts both home and public life (Genesis 3:16; 1 Corinthians 11:13; Ephesians 5:22; Colossians 3:18). As the "god of this world" (2 Corinthians 4:4), he promotes humanism and godless materialism, perverts the Scriptures, opposes God's program, hinders the Gospel and works lying wonders (2 Thessalonians 2:4, 9; 2 Peter 2:1).

Like a "roaring lion … seeking whom he may devour" (1 Peter 5:8), he walks to and fro in the earth, entices the Lord's children to sin and accuses them before God (Job 1:6–11; Revelation 12:10). He is the father of lies (John 8:44) and would, if possible, deceive the very elect. This incorrigible derelict is just as crafty as he is wicked.

Knowing man's utter depravity without God, Satan strikes where he can wreak the greatest havoc. One of his master moves was taking the Bible and prayer out of the schoolroom and replacing them with man's theories of evolution and a

---

[1]Since women began to undress before the public gaze, men have regressed to the bestial character of the cavemen. Like Adam and Eve, they are fully conscious of their sin, but cunningly hide behind the fig-leaf of social acceptance.

socialistic program, which cultivates the baser nature of the child and creates within him an animalistic, godless point of view. The train of evil that followed in the wake of this action is legion, for here was the seedbed, which gave birth to juvenile delinquency and rebellion against authority.

The church is Satan's prime target, and he seeks in every way possible to destroy its witness and testimony. With artful mockery, he perpetrates a union of the true body of Christ and the world by sowing tares (his own children) within the church membership and setting up a formal, ritualistic type of ceremonialism, which renders it lukewarm and lifeless.

> "Having a form of godliness, but denying the power thereof …" (2 Timothy 3:5).

He then stalks the aisles of the sanctuary, winking at the wretched, miserable, poor, blind, naked condition of its membership.

He exploits the sanctity of Christian womanhood with his popular ideal of the lovely, talented young girl who frequents the discotheque or competes in a bathing beauty contest on Saturday night and makes the sanctuary ring with "All On the Altar for Jesus" on Sunday morning.

He has succeeded in turning our Lord's Day into a day of pleasure and commercialization, the sacredness of Easter into a fashion parade, and Christmas into a hilarious holiday of fun and frolic and the idolizing of a pagan Santa Claus.

He empties our church pews on Sunday mornings by promoting his own sophisticated gods, such as sports, concerts, nature worship, and all of the ramifications of human endeavors, which provide temporary satisfaction for the soul but leave one bereft of spiritual power to cope with the situations of life.

Satan has a bag full of tricks, and most of them involve the **ego**. Man is so enamored with himself, and so intent upon satisfying his fleshly desires from the cradle to the grave, that he becomes easy prey to anything that smacks of self-gratification. Working through "the lust of the flesh, and the lust of the eyes, and the pride of life" (1 John 2:16, 17), he has the great stream of humanity following in his train to the brink of destruction.

Chapter 13
WORLDLY WISDOM

Satan dispenses his own brand of knowledge and wisdom which the Bible calls "the wisdom of this world" (1 Cor. 1:20). It knows nothing of God and functions independently of Him. This **worldly wisdom** has its very source in **Satan**, the **god and prince** of this world-system (2 Corinthians 4:4; John 14:30). Although it may acknowledge God as Creator and Sustainer of the universe, it rejects His counsel and runs counter to His moral and ethical standards.

It is the wisdom of earthly princes and potentates, who continually crucify the Lord of glory by ignoring His precepts and thereby denying Him the right to rule over His own creation. It puts man on the throne and demotes God to the status of a mere spectator of world events, who rallies to the support of every political and religious move made by the patron saints.

This is the **wisdom** with which Satan enticed Eve in the Garden of Eden. His subtle temptation was a challenge to her intellect, an invitation to partake of a sinister type of knowledge and wisdom, which God in His infinite love had forbidden. The promised reward for disobedience was overwhelming in scope:

> "... your eyes shall be opened, and ye shall be as gods, knowing good and evil" (Genesis 3:5).

Fired with uncontrollable curiosity and driven by an insatiable desire for the mysterious unknown, the woman reached forth her hand to pluck and to eat of the forbidden fruit. So delightful was the sensation, that she offered it to her husband, who also ate of it. Suddenly, a miraculous change came over them. God's Spirit was withdrawn, their **eyes were opened**, there was **instant perception**, and **new dimensions** of **knowledge**, **reason** and **imagination** were now available to them. They **saw**, they **knew**, not only good, but also **evil**. The curse of Satan's power was upon them and they became subservient to **death** and **depravity**.

This primeval event involved much, much more than a mere act of disobedience. Possibly, the tree of knowledge of good and evil was the end product of Satan's extensive experimentations in the field of horticulture prior to his rebellion. The fruit, laden with some mysterious virus, brought about an instantaneous change in the chemical makeup of their minds and bodies.

Overcome by Satan's powerful injection, they were now knowledgeable in forbidden avenues of thinking and acting, and as a consequence, they became the progenitors of a race of worldly-wise, self-seeking homosapiens, separated from God and in need of redemption.

Here, then, is the source of man's depravity, a naturalistic way of thinking and reasoning, which fills the mind with deceptive ideologies, false hopes and false values. In modern vernacular, it is termed intellectualism, scientism, rationalism and humanism. It elevates the basest of men to the status of the gods. It arrogantly inquires into the secrets of God's universe and attempts to build its own star by directing the course of nature and of history.

Highly prized and sought after in our great institutions of learning, this fallacious type of wisdom has become a god in itself. It is proud, rebellious humanity, bypassing the only true God with its high-sounding rhetoric, philosophic surmising and egotistical pursuits.

> "This wisdom descendeth not from above, but *is* earthly, sensual, devilish. For where envying and strife *is*, there *is* confusion and every evil work" (James 3:15, 16).

Countless civilizations have risen to power on the strength of Satan's elusive promises, only to crumble into the dust of their hopes and ideas. Some have retained God in their thoughts for a space of time, only to succumb in the end to internal corruption and moral decay and go the way of all nations that forget God (Psalm 9:17).

Our present civilization, built upon military might, racial prestige and a fluctuating monetary system, is dangerously tottering on the brink of self-destruction. Collapse is inevitable, and down will go the epitome of man's delusive dreams.

Every generation has produced its great philosophers and technologists who have sought to know the mind of God through human logic and deduction. But since man by worldly wisdom cannot find God, neither can know Him (Job 11:7; 1 Corinthians 1:21), it becomes his deadly enemy, cutting him off from his only source of redemption, and reducing him to the rank of a helpless reprobate.

Understandably, God has nothing but condemnation for that which is satanic and totally destructive. Because of His infinite love for humanity and hatred for that which would destroy him, He determines to bring to naught the wisdom of this world.

> "For it is written, I will destroy the wisdom of the wise, and will bring to nothing the understanding of the prudent. Where *is* the wise? where *is* the scribe? where *is* the disputer of this world? hath not God made foolish the wisdom of this world?" (1 Corinthians 1:19, 20).

> "Let no man deceive himself. If any man among you seemeth to be wise in this world, let him become a fool, that he may be wise. For the wisdom of this world is foolishness with God. For it is written, He taketh the wise in their own craftiness" (1 Corinthians 3:18, 19).

By way of glorious contrast, God offers to man His own infinite wisdom from above, which is

> "… first pure, then peaceable, gentle, *and* easy to be intreated, full of mercy and good fruits, without partiality, and without hypocrisy" (James 3:17).

This God-given, Spirit-transmitted wisdom is vested in Christ, "In whom are hid all the treasures of wisdom and knowledge" (Colossians 2:3) and is available to all who will receive His word into their minds and hearts.

> "For the LORD giveth wisdom: out of his mouth *cometh* knowledge and understanding" (Proverbs 2:6).

It is an indisputable fact that worldly wisdom is under the judgment of God and will come to naught. But man would rather set his own course, direct his own steps, build his own star, and go down into oblivion, than stay within the orbit of the lowly pathway of love and service hewn out by his Creator and Redeemer.

Chapter 14
SATAN'S KINGDOMS

Satan has built kingdom after kingdom, only to have them fall to pieces and decay from internal depravity and corruption. Four of his kingdoms have been worldwide in scope and comprise Gentile world rule, which began with the reign of Nebuchadnezzar and will end with the reign of the Antichrist at the close of this present age.

Nebuchadnezzar was given a vision in which these four world kingdoms (empires) were portrayed in the form of a great image (Daniel 2:31–34). Later, they were revealed to the prophet Daniel in the form of four beasts (Daniel 7:1–23). The image portrayed their outward splendor, while the beasts revealed their inward character. The two visions blend perfectly, and reveal that the four world kingdoms were to rise and fall successively, and in the fall of the fourth and last one, Gentile world rule would be brought to a dramatic close.

The prophecies of the first three of these empires were fulfilled in Babylon, Media-Persia, and Greece, all of which have been seen to take form, rise to world domination, and meet with deterioration and decay through the natural channels of weakness, which characterize all human institutions.

The prophecies relating to the fourth and last kingdom pertain to the old Roman Empire whose political and religious practices have never died out but have continued to smolder down through the centuries. Although Rome ceased to exist as a world power in the year AD 365, fragments of its autocratic framework still remain to this day and will come to life again in the form of a ten-king federation under one supreme dictator.

The fourth great world kingdom, symbolized by the feet and toes of the image and the fourth beast of Daniel's vision (Daniel 2:31–43; 7:1–12), is now in formation, but will not be in full manifestation until the very end of the present age, at which time the world will be under the complete control of "that man of sin," the Antichrist.

The visions reveal that it is to be diverse from all other kingdoms which have preceded it and "shall devour the whole earth, and shall tread it down, and break it in pieces" (Daniel 7:23). It is to be "dreadful and terrible, and strong exceedingly" (Daniel 7:7); "strong as iron: forasmuch as iron breaketh in pieces and subdueth all *things*" (Daniel 2:40).

A nearer vision of this same kingdom is found in Revelation 13, where a beast is seen to rise up out of the sea (populace), having seven heads and ten horns "and the dragon [Satan] gave him his power, and his seat, and great authority … And he opened his mouth in blasphemy against God, to blaspheme his name, and his tabernacle, and them that dwell in heaven … and power was given him over all kindreds, and tongues, and nations. And all that dwell upon the earth shall worship him, whose names are not written in the book of life of the Lamb slain from the foundation of the world" (Revelation 13:2–8).

This is a picture of the last great world-system in its final stage. The ten horns and ten crowns represent a ten-nation federation and its leaders who will receive power under the

Antichrist for a short duration but later become mere figureheads as he becomes the supreme authority. Both the system and its head are in view here. They are so inseparably bound together that they appear as one.

It is in the days of these kings that the God of heaven is to set up a kingdom, which shall "break in pieces and consume all these kingdoms, and it shall stand for ever" (Daniel 2:44). "And the kingdom and dominion, and the greatness of the kingdom under the whole heaven, shall be given to the people of the saints of the most High, whose kingdom *is* an everlasting kingdom, and all dominions shall serve and obey him" (Daniel 7:27).

How then, **when** and **in what manner** is this to be brought about? Let us note to begin with, that the change is consummated, not through a gradual conversion of the kingdoms of this world into the kingdom of God, but through the utter annihilation of the former prior to the establishment of the latter. This is revealed in the vision of the great image in which a "stone was cut out without hands" (Daniel2:34) is seen to smite the image (Gentile world-system) upon its feet and its composite parts: the iron, the clay, the brass, the silver, and the gold are broken into pieces together and become like the chaff of the summer threshingfloor and carried away with the wind. Then the **stone** cut out without hands is seen to become a great mountain (kingdom) and fill the whole earth (Daniel 2:35). Thus, it is evident that the complete destruction of present Gentile world-power is inevitable and unavoidable. But what is the outside force, the **stone** cut out without hands, which brings about its destruction? The **stone** is a symbol of Christ. In Matthew 21:42, Jesus likens Himself to "the stone which the builders rejected," and proclaims that it became "the head of the corner" or **chief cornerstone**. Then He adds, "whosoever shall fall on this stone shall be broken: but on whomsoever it shall fall, it will grind him to powder" (Matthew 21:44).

Both Israel and the Roman Empire fell upon the **stone** when they crucified the Savior, both being equally guilty of the offense, and just as the nation Israel was broken up and dispersed throughout the world, so was the power and spirit of the Roman Empire broken to pieces and eventually scattered to the ends of the earth.

Ancient history lists Christianity as one of the chief causes of the decline and fall of the ancient Roman Empire. It records that as the Christian religion took hold on the populace and spread throughout the Empire, the new converts were naturally hostile toward a government and society based on idolatry. Gradually, they began to undermine the worn-out parts of the old system and to impress their own character on what remained.[1]

Then too, many of the rulers came under the influence of Christian teachings. Constantine even professed the new faith (although he remained more pagan than "Christian" in character), and raised Christianity to an equal footing with paganism. The "Church" and State were united, the absolute sovereignty of the Emperor gave way to the popular will, and the unrelenting iron rule began to lose its grip, being no longer able to enslave its subjects. Soon afterwards the disintegration of the Roman Empire was accomplished.

Thus, the "deadly wound" was inflicted to this great and seemingly impregnable fortress (Satan's head on earth) by

---

[1] *An Ancient History for Beginners*, by G.W. Botsford.

the introduction of Christianity within its borders. Revelation 13:3 tells us that this **head** (the Roman Empire) which received the deadly wound, is to be revived toward the end of the age and will come under the domination of a supreme ruler, that "man of sin" (2 Thessalonians 2:3,8–10), who will be promoted by the False Prophet (a religious figurehead). The ten-nation federation of European powers under the label "Common Market" and the almost universal popularity of the papacy, could well be the beginning of the fulfillment of this prophecy.

Israel will be drawn into the maelstrom of end-time events by her strategic location and her unpopularity with most peoples of the world. According to God's Word, she is destined to be the vortex of the final conflagration.

Chapter 15
GOD'S CONTROVERSY WITH THE NATIONS

"... the LORD hath a controversy with the nations, he will plead with all flesh; he will give them *that are* wicked to the sword, saith the LORD. Thus saith the LORD of hosts, Behold, evil shall go forth from nation to nation, and a great whirlwind shall be raised up from the coasts of the earth. And the slain of the LORD shall be at that day from *one* end of the earth even unto the *other* end of the earth ..." (Jeremiah 25:31–33).

"... the LORD hath a controversy with the inhabitants of the land, because *there is* no truth, nor mercy, nor knowledge of God in the land. By swearing, and lying, and killing, and stealing, and committing adultery, they break out, and blood toucheth blood. Therefore shall the land mourn, and every one that dwelleth therein shall languish ..." (Hosea 4:1–3).

"For, behold, the day cometh, that shall burn as an oven; and all the proud, yea, and all that do wickedly, shall be stubble: and the day that cometh shall burn them up, saith the LORD of hosts, that it shall leave them neither root nor branch" (Malachi 4:1).

> "... I will call for a sword upon all the inhabitants of the earth, saith the LORD of hosts ... Out of the north an evil shall break forth upon all the inhabitants of the land" (Jeremiah 25:29; 1:14).

> "... for my determination *is* to gather the nations, that I may assemble the kingdoms, to pour upon them mine indignation, *even* all my fierce anger: for all the earth shall be devoured with the fire of my jealousy" (Zephaniah 3:8).

Is God angry? Yes, "God is angry *with the wicked* every day" (Psalm 7:11), and He will surely recompense evil for evil in the coming Day of Wrath. "Because he hath appointed a day, in the which he will judge the world in righteousness by *that* man whom he hath ordained; ... in that he hath raised him from the dead" (Acts 17:31).

The **fire** was kindled and the **sword** drawn with the first coming of Christ into the world. The event of the birth of the baby Jesus set in motion a progression of events, which led to His trial and crucifixion and is destined to end in the tearing down and breaking in pieces of the entire present world system. Speaking through the prophet, Ezekiel, the Lord says,

> "I will overturn, overturn, overturn, it: and it shall be no *more*, until he come whose right it is; and I will give it *him*" (Ezekiel 21:27).

> "Son of man, prophesy, and say, Thus saith the LORD; Say, A sword, a sword is sharpened, and also furbished ... and let the sword be doubled the third time ..." (Ezekiel 21:9, 14).

Can we very well deny that the **three overturns** and **thrice doubling of the sword** began with **World War I**? Is there any substantial evidence against **World War II** being the second overturn and twice the doubling of the sword? Indeed, it would be difficult to find words that more adequately describe those two great world conflagrations, which destroyed kingdoms, shuffled boundaries, scattered nationalities and changed the whole course of civilization. We dare say that only the woefully ignorant and spiritually blind would deny the probability of their being a direct fulfillment of God's prophecy concerning the **end of Gentile world rule**.

Conceding then the probability of our having witnessed the first two overturns, where do we now stand in world history? Shall we be honest enough to suppose that we are on the very brink of the consummation of the age, with the final overturn hanging like a death pall over every country of the globe?

The third and **final overturn** will involve every nation of the world in a **global confrontation**, the likes of which man has never before experienced. All will end in the Battle of Armageddon where blood will flow to a depth of the horses' bridles and vultures will flock from the four winds of heaven to clean up the stench (Revelation 19:17–19).

The land of Palestine will be the vortex of this bloody conflict, and the **return of Christ in glory** from heaven with His armies will determine the final outcome. A vision of this was given to the apostle John on the Isle of Patmos and can be found in Revelation 14:14–20 and 19:11–21. Present day stockpiling of nuclear weapons and the mobilization of military power by the more aggressive nations are clear indications of what lies ahead.

Chapter 16
THE DAY OF GOD'S WRATH

> "The great day of the LORD *is* near, *it is* near, and hasteth greatly …" (Zephaniah 1:14).

> "Behold, the day of the LORD cometh, cruel both with wrath and fierce anger …" (Isaiah 13:9).

> "Fear, and the pit, and the snare, *are* upon thee, O inhabitant of the earth" (Isaiah 24:17).

Yea, even now the great and terrible **Day of the Lord**, the **day of His vengeance** is approaching like a great whirlwind—**overturning**, **overturning**, **overturning**—taking unprecedented toll of life and property and gaining momentum with each overturn.

> "That day *is* a day of wrath, a day of trouble and distress, a day of wasteness and desolation, a day of darkness and gloominess, a day of clouds and thick darkness …" (Zephaniah 1:15).

> "For the stars of heaven and the constellations thereof shall not give their light: the sun shall be darkened in his going forth, and the moon shall not cause her light to shine. And I will punish the world for *their* evil,

> and the wicked for their iniquity; and I will cause the arrogancy of the proud to cease, and will lay low the haughtiness of the terrible. I will make a man more precious than fine gold; even a man than the golden wedge of Ophir. Therefore I will shake the heavens, and the earth shall remove out of her place, in the wrath of the LORD of hosts, and in the day of his fierce anger" (Isaiah 13:10–13).

> "And I will bring distress upon men, that they shall walk like blind men, because they have sinned against the LORD: and their blood shall be poured out as dust, and their flesh as the dung. Neither their silver nor their gold shall be able to deliver them in the day of the LORD'S wrath; but the whole land shall be devoured by the fire of his jealousy …" (Zephaniah 1:17, 18).

All creation is now travailing under the curse, and tribulation is the lot of all humanity from birth to the grave. Yet the Bible clearly designates a special time in history in which the world will experience distress and disaster in unprecedented proportions.

About 500 BC, the prophet Daniel made the following prediction concerning end-time events:

> "… and there shall be a time of trouble, such as never was since there was a nation *even* to that same time …" (Daniel 12:1).

Jesus verified and intensified this prophecy. In a lengthy discourse on the escalation of end-time events, He summed it all up in these words:

> "For then shall be great tribulation, such as was not since the beginning of the world to this time, no, nor ever shall be" (Matthew 24:21).

This dreadful time of sorrow and confusion has aptly been called "seven years of **hell on earth**." Beginning with the opening of the seven seals (Revelation 6:1–8:6), and ending with the **Battle of Armageddon** (Revelation 16:13–16), it will overtake the unsuspecting world with a sudden irremediable blow, as a **destruction** from the **Almighty** (Joel 1:15).

> "For, behold, the LORD will come with fire, and with his chariots like a whirlwind, to render his anger with fury, and his rebuke with flames of fire. For by fire and by his sword will the LORD plead with all flesh: and the slain of the LORD shall be many" (Isaiah 66:15, 16).

This will be a period of rapid, violent changes in the earth's surface and weather patterns caused by cosmological upheavals affecting the stratosphere. All nature will seem to go on a rampage. Earthquakes, hurricanes, tornadoes, floods, droughts, hail, and electrical storms will be greatly multiplied and intensified. War, famine and plagues will follow in their wake. What we are witnessing today is only the "beginning of sorrows" (Matthew 24:8), a mere sample of what is to come when the Tribulation strikes with full force.

Utter chaos will reign throughout the world as the forces of evil are unleashed upon the unrepentant hordes of Christ-rejectors. Demons will flock to the earth in unrestrained legions, taking possession of men's minds and bodies, filling them with lust and greed and passion such as no generation has ever yet experienced. Every man will be against his brother and the entire earth will be filled with hatred, violence and corruption.

Great swarms of unearthly creatures with scorpion-like tails and 200 million horsemen venting streams of fire and brimstone will be released from the bottomless pit to compass the earth, tormenting men with their scorpion-like tails, and destroying one-third of the world's population (Revelation 9:1–18).

Rivers and fountains will be filled with blood, darkness will cover the land, and men's bodies will be covered with sores and scorched with heat until they will gnaw their tongues for pain and cry out for the rocks and mountains to fall on them (Revelation 6:16, 17; 16:1–10).

The fire of God's wrath is to be literally poured out upon the earth during this period, causing it "reel to and fro like a drunkard" (Isaiah 24:20), and to be shaken from center to circumference with lightnings, thunders, earthquakes, and hailstones the size of a talent (fifty to 100 pounds), bringing to task everything of an unrighteous nature, and causing men's hearts to fail them "for fear, and for looking after those things which are coming on the earth: for the powers of heaven shall be shaken" (Luke 21:26).

> "And I will shew wonders in the heavens and in the earth, blood, and fire, and pillars of smoke. The sun shall be turned into darkness, and the moon into blood, before the great and the terrible day of the LORD come. And it shall come to pass, *that* whosoever shall call on the name of the LORD shall be delivered" (Joel 2:30–32).

All of these manifestations of supernatural power will strike terror into the hearts of men and cause many to turn to the Lord and be saved from eternal doom.

Throughout the entire Tribulation period, God will send out repeated warnings and give chance after chance to men to repent, and a **great multitude** consisting of both Jews and Gentiles will turn to Him and be saved for eternity (Revelation 7:9–17).

However, these will not escape the **wrath** of the **Antichrist, who will at that time have supreme power over the nations of the earth** and make the demand that all mankind worship the image of himself. All who refuse to do so will pay with their lives. They will be slain for the Word of God and for their testimony (Revelation 7:1–17; 6:9–11).

> "… they shall fall by the sword, and by flame, by captivity, and by spoil, *many* days … And *some* of them of understanding shall fall, to try them, and to purge, and to make *them* white, *even* to the time of the end …" (Daniel 11:33, 35).

These are the Tribulation saints of Revelation 7:9–17, where we see a great multitude of people from every nation and kindred and tribe standing before the throne of God, wearing white robes, and with palms in their hands. They are clearly identified as "they which came out of great tribulation, and have washed their robes, and made them white in the blood of the Lamb" (Revelation 7:14).

Although they can never be a part of the body and bride of Christ, they will enjoy perfect bliss throughout eternity as they serve God day and night in His temple. They constitute the unprepared virgins of Matthew 25:1–10 and the unprofitable servants of Matthew 24:51 and 25:30.

God's purpose in all of His dealings with humanity is to bring them to repentance and prepare them for an eternity with Him. Yet, after all of His pleadings and purgings, we read that "the rest of the men which were not killed by these plagues yet repented not of the works of their hands, that they should not worship devils, and idols of gold, and silver, and brass, and stone, and of wood: which neither can see, nor hear, nor walk: Neither repented they of their murders, nor of their sorceries, nor of their fornication, nor of their thefts" (Revelation 9:20, 21).

What God cannot salvage, He must destroy. The very righteousness of God requires the annihilation of all ungodliness in the earth. Although He is longsuffering "not willing that any should perish, but that all should come to repentance" (2 Peter 3:9), He will surely bring all men to an accounting, for the **wrath of God abideth** on them that **believe not the Son** (John 3:36).

Yet the world will not accept the fact of God's vindictive hatred of sin and His holy determination to make an end of it, but after their hardness and impenitent hearts, they treasure up "wrath against the day of wrath," by their ungodliness and unbelief (Rom. 2:5). There is only one way to escape this terrible wrath to come. First Thessalonians 5:9 says, "For God hath not appointed us to wrath, but to obtain salvation by our Lord Jesus Christ …." Jesus Christ took the cup of wrath for us at Calvary, therefore, if we are "in Christ" as born-again believers, we will be raptured out of this world before the Great Tribulation, just as Enoch was taken out before Noah's flood (Genesis 5:24). If you do not want to face the wrath of Almighty God, then receive His Son as your personal Saviour. Good works, church membership, moral living, good intentions, sincerity, and religion will do you no good in the day of God's wrath. You must be born again. (See John 3:1–3; Acts 16:31; Ephesians 2:8–10; Romans 10:9–13; John 14:6; and Galatians 2:16.)

Jesus pointed out the two ways that are open unto all men everywhere during this age of grace. He said:

> "Enter ye in at the strait gate: for wide *is* the gate, and broad *is* the way, that leadeth to destruction, and many there be which go in thereat: Because strait *is* the gate, and narrow *is* the way, which leadeth unto life, and few there be that find it" (Matthew 7:13, 14).

Chapter 17
THE ANTICHRIST AND ARMAGEDDON

> "Let no man deceive you by any means: for *that day shall not come*, except there come a falling away first, and that man of sin be revealed, the son of perdition; Who opposeth and exalteth himself above all that is called God, or that is worshipped; so that he as God sitteth in the temple of God, shewing himself that he is God … *Even him*, whose coming is after the working of Satan with all power and signs and lying wonders …" (2 Thessalonians 2:3, 4, 9).

No doubt, Satan's alter-ego is now in the final stages of development, and he will suddenly make his appearance on the world stage at the appointed time. Some great universal crisis will strike with lightning force, throwing the existing monetary and political systems into a state of total chaos, and driven by the fear of anarchy and complete annihilation, all nations will be brought under the **dictatorship of one supreme head.** Speaking with great swelling words and posing as a friend of man and the "saviour" of the world, this brilliant, illustrious diplomat will win the favor and admiration of all nationalities by his superb strategy in solving the world's knotty problems.

Heading up a ten-nation confederacy, such as the now existing European Common Market, this charismatic genius will astound the world with his military prowess and promotional schemes. His magnetic personality and superhuman qualities of leadership will capture the popular imagination and inspire unswerving devotion and allegiance to himself and his program, so that when he and his henchman (the False Prophet of Revelation 13) come with their miraculous schemes for a perfect social order, coupled with ostentatious demonstrations of power over the elements (such as bringing fire down from heaven and maneuvering weather conditions), the world will receive him with open arms.

By this time, science and technology will have advanced to the stage where man will think himself to have mastered the secrets of the universe, and it will be through the use of spectacular scientific exhibitions and the rationing of the world's food stuffs and other resources, that the Antichrist will exercise control over all humanity. With major world powers already vying for a show of military might in space, the issue of supremacy may soon be resolved and the Antichrist revealed.

> "And the king shall do according to his will; and he shall exalt himself, and magnify himself above every god, and shall speak marvellous things against the God of gods … Neither shall he regard the God of his fathers, nor the desire of women, nor regard any god: for he shall magnify himself above all. But in his estate shall he honour the God of forces: and a god whom his fathers knew not shall he honour with gold, and silver, and with precious stones, and pleasant things" (Daniel 11:36–38).

> "And he doeth great wonders, so that he maketh fire come down from heaven on the earth in the sight of men, And deceiveth them that dwell on the earth by *the means of* those miracles which he had power to do in the sight of the beast ... And he had power to give life unto the image of the beast, that the image of the beast should both speak, and cause that as many as would not worship the image of the beast should be killed. And he causeth all, both small and great, rich and poor, free and bond, to receive a mark in their right hand, or in their foreheads: And that no man might buy or sell, save he that had the mark, or the name of the beast, or the number of his name ... and his number *is* Six hundred threescore *and* six" (Revelatian 13:13–18).

The number "six" in Biblical usage is the number of man, and the triple digit "666" denotes the ultimate in human development without God. The Antichrist will be the epitome of the humanist ideal. The television screen, the popularity poll, the beauty pageant and the talent show—all have contributed to the erection of a pedestal from which this egomaniac will win the applause of the populace and will set up his reign of glamorous terror. For though outwardly charming, he is a **bestial monster**, the very incarnation of Satan himself.

Bestiality is a glaring trait of this twentieth century generation. The growing popularity of horror movies, and the complacent acceptance of the violence and sex portrayed on stage and screen, brand us as an immoral, bestial type of society.

Satan's demoralization and dehumanization program is progressing at full speed, and all is in preparation for that approaching day when the living, breathing, speaking image of the Beast of Revelation 13 makes his appearance and demands total obedience.

Henry Spaak, one of the drafters of the European Common Market, revealed the heart of the masses in one of his speeches in 1974, when he said, "What we want is a man of sufficient stature to hold the allegiance of our people, and to lift us out of the economic morass into which we are sinking. Send us such a man and, **be he God or Devil,** we will receive him."

We are living in the day of the glorification of the flesh, and the world is looking for its ideal to idolize. So when this charismatic superman comes on the scene, he will easily capture the hearts of the people with his majestic bearing and oratorical genius. This wanton old world will stand at attention and give him its allegiance. This will no doubt be manipulated through the positioning of huge television screens set up at strategic locations throughout the cities and towns of all nations.

Jesus said to His people, Israel, "I am come in my Father's name, and ye receive me not: if another shall come in his own name, him ye will receive" (John 5:43). Israel is still looking for her Messiah and earthly kingdom, and when this great deceiver appears impersonating the Messiah and magnifying himself under the pretense of being their deliverer, the Jews will receive him as their God-appointed Saviour.

In an attempt to usurp the throne of the Son of God, he will give the order to restore and rebuild the temple, make a covenant with the Jews for the restoration of their temple worship, and even sit in the temple of God showing himself that he is God (2 Thessalonians 2:4).

This "king of fierce countenance" (Daniel 8:23) and usurper of Christ's throne will be permitted to reign and prosper and practice his weird deception for a short space of time, and although much of the world's population will be experiencing untold misery and martyrdom, the majority will render him obeisance and revel in the fruits of his prosperity.

The Golden Age, which man has so long dreamed of, will appear to have arrived. All industrial, political, commercial, and social activities will be highly accelerated and multiplied. Gold and silver will be in plentiful supply, and man's lust for materialism and sensuality will be gratified in the fullest possible measure (Daniel 8:23–25).

Either the ancient city of Babylon will be rebuilt, or some existing metropolis will impersonate her and become the nucleus of all the world's trade, and of traffickers in the souls of men. Called the **MOTHER OF HARLOTS** AND **ABOMINATIONS OF THE EARTH** (Revelation 17:5), she will transcend anything the world has ever known in power and wealth and every form of sensuous entertainment. The entire city will be given over to riotous, unrestrained lust, occultism, Satan worship, drug traffic, drinking and gambling. A city of eternal day, it will make Monte Carlo and Las Vegas look like theater sets by comparison. Fast moving planes and elaborate networks of speedways will transport illustrious entertainers and greedy patrons from all over the world to indulge in the hilarious sensuality of its night clubs and pornographic entertainment.

Although God's angels will continue to bombard the earth with unrelenting regularity during this period, much of the destruction will no doubt be localized as great metropolitan areas, and even entire nations, come under the judgment of Almighty God.

In spite of these judgments, which will be viewed as mere meteorological disturbances, the Antichrist will be given plenty of rope, and man will be given his one last opportunity to build his cherished utopian world order, this time without interference from the Holy Spirit who will have been taken out of the way at the time of the Rapture (2 Thessalonians 2:6, 7). Under the complete control of Satan's puppet monarch, the world will experience a short period of enforced peace and feigned prosperity.

But blundering, rebellious, sinful humanity, left to follow the inclinations of his own wicked, unrestrained heart, will bungle his last chance, and all will go down the drain when Israel discovers the true identity of her false Messiah and refuses to worship him. From then on, it is pandemonium all the way to the end, as he turns on the Jewish nation and seeks to banish them from the face of the earth. As a result of his atrocious persecutions of God's chosen people, the whole world will become embroiled in continuous conflict.

The fall of Babylon will be sudden and without remedy. A great earthquake will rip its foundations from center to circumference (Revelation 16:18, 19), and the entire city, with its millions of revelling occupants, will sink into a molten lake of flaming bitumen which lies beneath the foundations of an ancient location. A description of this awful destruction can be found in Revelation 18.

The grand finale to Satan's usurpation of God's earthly domain will be brought about by the third and final event of world history—**the Battle of Armageddon** (Revelation 14:14–20; 16:13, 14).

> "And I saw three unclean spirits like frogs *come* out of the mouth of the dragon [Satan], and out of the mouth of the beast [Antichrist], and out of the mouth

> of the false prophet [false religious leader]. For they are the spirits of devils, working miracles, *which* go forth unto the kings of the earth and of the whole world, to gather them to the battle of that great day of God Almighty … And he gathered them together into a place called in the Hebrew tongue Armageddon" (Revelation 16:13–14, 16).

> "And the angel thrust in his sickle into the earth, and gathered the vine of the earth, and cast *it* into the great winepress of the wrath of God. And the winepress was trodden without the city, and blood came out of the winepress, even unto the horse bridles, by the space of a thousand *and* six hundred furlongs" (Revelation 14:19, 20).

Simultaneous with this great slaughter of opposing armies, will be the sudden appearance of **Christ** and **His armies from heaven** to complete the destruction of His enemies.

> "And I saw heaven opened, and behold a white horse; and he that sat upon him *was* called Faithful and True, and in righteousness he doth judge and make war … And out of his mouth goeth a sharp sword, that with it he should smite the nations: and he shall rule them with a rod of iron: and he treadeth the winepress of the fierceness and wrath of Almighty God … And I saw the beast, and the kings of the earth, and their armies, gathered together to make war against him that sat on the horse, and against his army. And the beast was taken, and with him the false prophet that wrought

> miracles before him, with which he deceived them that had received the mark of the beast, and them that worshipped his image. These both were cast alive into a lake of fire burning with brimstone. And the remnant were slain with the sword of him that sat upon the horse, which *sword* proceeded out of his mouth: and all the fowls were filled with their flesh" (Revelation 19:11, 15, 19–21).

Right on the heels of this great massacre, an angel will descend from Heaven with a key to the bottomless pit and a great chain in his hand.

> "And he laid hold on the dragon, that old serpent, which is the Devil, and Satan, and bound him a thousand years, And cast him into the bottomless pit, and shut him up, and set a seal upon him, that he should deceive the nations no more, till the thousand years should be fulfilled …" (Revelation 20:2, 3).

Chapter 18
THE GREAT UPSWEEP

Only for the truly born-again believer is there hope for deliverance from the approaching holocaust, for "God hath not appointed us to wrath, but to obtain salvation by our Lord Jesus Christ" (1 Thessalonians 5:9). Our Lord and Saviour, Jesus Christ, has promised to make a way of escape for His redeemed. He has committed Himself to the stupendous task of delivering us bodily from the onslaught of the great devastation that is coming upon all the earth. Speaking to His disciples just before His departure for heaven, He said: "I go to prepare a place for you. And if I go and prepare a place for you, I will come again, and receive you unto myself; that where I am, *there* ye may be also" (John 14:2, 3).

One day, when the stock markets are soaring and the freeways are buzzing with traffic—when people are eating and drinking, buying and selling, planting and reaping, marrying and giving in marriage—when everything seems to be rocking along at its usual pace of turmoil and confusion—Christ will come for His bride!

A brilliant flash of lightning will encircle the entire globe as the glorified Christ suddenly appears in mid-heaven with a shout of victory and a blast of the trumpet. In the same instant, all of the redeemed in Christ will mysteriously disappear from earth's troubled scene.

"For the Lord himself shall descend from heaven with a shout, with the voice of the archangel, and with the trump of God: and the dead in Christ shall rise first: Then we which are alive *and* remain shall be caught up together with them in the clouds, to meet the Lord in the air: and so shall we ever be with the Lord" (1 Thessalonians 4:16, 17).

"Behold, I shew you a mystery; We shall not all sleep, but we shall all be changed, In a moment, in the twinkling of an eye, at the last trump: for the trumpet shall sound, and the dead shall be raised incorruptible, and we shall be changed. For this corruptible must put on incorruption, and this mortal *must* put on immortality. So when this corruptible shall have put on incorruption, and this mortal shall have put on immortality, then shall be brought to pass the saying that is written, Death is swallowed up in victory" (1 Corinthians 15:51–54).

Picture this in your mind: A point of light! A billowy cloud! A trumpet blast! A shout of victory! And instantaneously, in the twinkling of an eye, without the rustle of a leaf or the lifting of a single clod of earth, all those who "sleep in Jesus" will be **quickened by the Spirit** and will spring forth from their silent tombs to **meet the Lord** in the **air!** In the same split second, the saved who are alive and remain on the earth will be caught up together with them in the clouds, taking on their glorified bodies in transit.

God's Word likens the resurrection body to that of a "corn of wheat," which springs forth from a tiny seed that has lain dormant in the cold, dark earth through the winter months (John 12:24). Then, when the spring rains come and the earth is warmed by the sun's rays, the dead, dry hull of the seed gives way to the life-germ within, and a beautiful plant bearing foliage and flowers springs forth to greet the eye of the beholder.

In like manner, the human body decays when God's Spirit is withdrawn at the time of physical death; but the life-giving germ (embryo) is retained and preserved until the day of Christ's return. At His appearance, the dormant seed will be quickened by the Spirit and will spring forth from the grave as an entirely new body—resembling the old, but electrified and glorified by the Spirit of God. (Read 1 Corinthians 15:35–49.) Christ, in rising from the grave, became the first-fruits of them that slept, and those who sleep in Christ will be resurrected in like manner at His coming.

The coming of Christ for His redeemed has also been likened to the drawing power of a magnet over certain metals of like properties. His feet will not touch ground, but while He remains momentarily suspended in mid-air, the drawing power of the Holy Spirit will attract only those of like Spirit, leaving behind the hoards of unbelievers to suffer the judgment of God. This is that "blessed hope," often referred to as the Rapture, for which Christians are admonished to watch, wait, and be ready (Titus 2:13). Like brands from the burning, we will be snatched out from among the scoffers and pretenders just before the Great Tribulation strikes in all its fury. O, mystery of mysteries! He who maketh the clouds His chariots and "walketh upon the wings of the wind" (Psalm 104:3), will put to shame all of man's puny space exploits when He comes in the clouds of glory to receive us to Himself, leaving a gaping world of doubters to wonder what has taken place.

However, an unbelieving, Christ-rejecting world could hardly be expected to be looking for a visit from God. If it were a prediction concerning a visit from the men of Mars, everything would be in readiness to receive them—but the Lord of Heaven!—that is a different matter! The main populace will be too preoccupied with earthly things to give heed to any prediction concerning the appearance of the Son of God. Being caught up in their own pursuits—the cares of the world and the deceitfulness of riches (Matthew 13:22)—they will even treat any warning with contempt and ridicule.

Let us not confuse the Rapture with Christ's coming in judgment at the end of the age. There are two phases of His Second Coming and these will be separated by a space of about seven years. All signs pertaining to His coming in judgment at the end of the seven-year Tribulation period, are given to warn the wicked of impending world catastrophe. However, since the redeemed are to be caught out seven years before His return, we can know by the signs now visible that the time is fast approaching for our deliverance. Once the Rapture has occurred, the door to the bridechamber will be shut (Matthew 25:10), and there will be no way of escaping the woes of the Tribulation period for those left behind. Every individual who has not received Jesus into his/her heart and life up to this point in time, will be left to suffer under the cruel and relentless hand of the Antichrist. This will include martyrdom for those who refuse to worship him or receive his mark (Revelation 13:15–17).

But the good news is that there is still time and opportunity to make preparation. The "Water of Life" is plentiful and available to all. One needs only to come to the risen Christ, accepting His love and forgiveness, and letting Him be Lord of his life. This means a whole new way of life. It means turning your back on the lusts of the world and following after righteousness, godliness and faith (Titus 2:12), for "If any man love the world, the love of the Father is not in him" (1 John 2:15). It means setting our affections on things above, not on things on the earth and living for God rather than for self-gratification (Philippians 2:5–8; Col. 3:2).

We are living in the dispensation of God's marvelous grace, during which time the Holy Spirit is wooing all mankind to come and drink of the water of life freely. Any and all who hear and heed the call to repentance and faith in the shed blood of Jesus, can partake of His Holy Spirit and be prepared for His coming. Christ's coming for His bride (the true church) is imminent. It is a signless, timeless, dateless event that could happen at any moment. Although on God's timetable man has no way of knowing the exact day nor hour it will happen, there is a definite point in world history for its occurrence. We only know that it will occur just prior to the seven-year Tribulation period, for Jesus has promised to deliver us from "the hour of temptation, which shall come upon all the world, to try them that dwell upon the earth" (Revelation 3:10).

NOTE: There are several different views concerning the rapture of the church. Some believe the church will go through the Tribulation, evidently ignoring the fact that there is no mention of the church anywhere in Revelation 4–18, where the Tribulation is described. Some believe the church will be raptured in the middle of the Tribulation. And even more farfetched are the ideas that there is no literal Tribulation to go through and no literal thousand-year millennium.

We are interested in only one view, and that is the Bible view. Too many doctrines are based on what a denomination teaches or even based on what some "scholar" has promoted. To determine the Bible view, we must first decide who or what makes up the church. We could go into great detail, but the Scripture does not require us to do so. Colossians 1:18–24 and Ephesians 1:22–23 make it abundantly clear that the church is the body of Christ. Ephesians 5:27–32 makes it clear that the church is the bride of Christ. Therefore, if you are part of the body of Christ, you are in the bride of Christ! How do you get in? Again, the Scriptures are clear. Acts 2:47 says, "And the Lord added to the church daily such as should be saved." So if you are saved, you are in **the church.** You should be active in a local church as is clear from the writings of Paul. However, you should be saved and, therefore, in the body of Christ before you join a local church. First Corinthians 12:13 says, "For by one Spirit are we all baptized into one body, whether *we be* Jews or Gentiles, whether *we be* bond or free; and have been all made to drink into one Spirit." If you are saved, you have the Holy Spirit (Romans 8:9), and it is the baptism of the Holy Spirit which accompanies salvation (Eph. 1:13) that places you in the body of Christ!

In summary, in order to get saved, you must receive the Lord Jesus Christ (John 1:12), and this places you in His body, the church. As you receive Jesus Christ, God places the Holy Spirit within you (1 Corinthians 3:16) to seal you (Ephesians 4:30), thereby preserving your salvation until He presents you to Himself as His bride! Now, why is this so important? Because as the body of Christ, you do not have to go to hell. Christ took your sin, your sufferings and your punishment for sin at Calvary. If Christ is in you, then He would go through the wrath of God a second time if we went through the Great Tribulation. It will not happen (1 Thessalonians 5:9–11)! **To God be the glory!**

Do not forget, the Great Tribulation is called the time of Jacob's (Israel's) trouble, not the time of the church's trouble. (See Jeremiah 30:7.) Praise God for mercy and grace on His church!

Chapter 19
THE RESIDUE

When Jesus removes His bride from the earth's scene, the world will be taken by surprise. Multitudes will be left behind to suffer the agonies of being separated from their loved ones, and the majority will have no perception of what has taken place. Pandemonium will reign as babies are snatched from their mother's arms and husbands and wives, sisters and brothers, parents and children, are separated with no apparent explanation.

When Enoch was "raptured," or translated, we read, "By faith Enoch was translated that he should not see death; and was not found, because God had translated him: for before his translation he had this testimony, that he pleased God" (Hebrews 11:5). After the Rapture, parents will be looking for their children, men will be looking for their wives, and some teenagers will be looking for their parents. But they will not be found. The Antichrist will no doubt have an explanation, perhaps saying it was the judgment of God on those Bible-thumping, fire-breathing, old-fashioned, fundamental fanatics. Whatever the case, the separation of the "saints" from the "aints" will be terrible for those left behind.

Imagine the scene throughout this overcrowded, overactivated world of people in which we live. Planes will crash to the ground, trains will jump their rails, and buses, trucks, and cars will pile up in snarling traffic jams as pilots and drivers are suddenly snatched from their seats. Homes will be vacated. Factories, supermarkets, ball parks, and other places of business and entertainment will be partially emptied, leaving multiplied millions of excited, bewildered patrons and customers to find their way back and to plunder over possessions abandoned by the raptured saints.

Newspapers will carry "Missing Persons" headlines and will attempt to solve the mysterious disappearances. There will be much speculation, but a generation that has thrived on space exploration and UFO sightings will not be completely knocked off their feet. Some will believe the missing ones have been whisked away by spaceships from another world, others will attribute it to some mishap in nuclear fission, while a third group will realize the significance of the event and start searching for a way to escape.

Many professing church members will wake up, only too late, to the truth of the situation. They will have heard the warnings of preachers and other born-again Christians concerning this very event but will have been too engrossed in worldly pursuits to give heed and make sufficient preparation.

They are represented by the foolish virgins in the parable of Matthew 25:1–13. They will have no oil[1] in their lamps when the bridegroom comes for His bride. The universal invitation to become a member of Christ's body will have ceased. The door to the "bridechamber" will then be closed, and the foolish virgins will be left on the outside seeking admittance. There will be weeping and wailing when they suddenly realize their plight—they must enter into the Great

---

[1]Oil in Bible usage is a symbol of the Holy Spirit.

Tribulation and endure their portion of punishment with the hypocrites and unbelievers (Matthew 13:22).

Jesus put it this way,

> "But and if that evil servant shall say in his heart, My lord delayeth his coming; And shall begin to smite *his* fellowservants, and to eat and drink with the drunken; The lord of that servant shall come in a day when he looketh not for *him*, and in an hour that he is not aware of, And shall cut him asunder, and appoint *him* his portion with the hypocrites: there shall be weeping and gnashing of teeth" (Matthew 24:48–51).

The same fate awaits those wicked and slothful servants who waste their talents by "hiding them in the earth,"[2] rather than investing them for the Lord's use. Jesus' pronouncement of condemnation is much the same: "… cast ye the unprofitable servant into outer darkness: there shall be weeping and gnashing of teeth" (Matthew 25:30).

> "And that servant, which knew his lord's will, and prepared not *himself*, neither did according to his will, shall be beaten with many *stripes*. But he that knew not, and did commit things worthy of stripes, shall be beaten with few *stripes*" (Luke 12:47, 48).

These are the multitudes who receive the seed (Word of God) by the wayside, or upon stony ground, or among thorns.

---

[2] Using one's talents for purely earthly (materialistic) gain or personal aggrandizement without regard for the Lord's will in one's life.

They hear the word and momentarily respond to its drawing power, but "then cometh the devil, and taketh away the word out of their hearts …" (Luke 8:12).

Through multiple trials and temptations, some fall away. In others, the word is choked with the **cares** and **pleasures** of life, and **the deceitfulness of riches**, and they become unfruitful (Matthew 13:19–22). Many of these grew up in Christian homes. They cut their teeth on Christian literature and church hymnals[3] and perhaps made professions of faith at an early age. But as they grew to adulthood, the pressures and temptations of the world overtook them, and they succumbed to "the lust of the flesh, and the lust of the eyes, and the pride of life …" (1 John 2:16). Even though some of them had submitted to water baptism, they had not experienced the new birth and had no power of resistance in themselves. Then, when the going got rough or the pull of the world's attractions overtook them, they had no strength to endure. Their superficial love for Christ waxed cold and they succumbed to the evil influences of society.

Others who have not heard the Gospel message and have no clear understanding of Christ's saving power, will receive less punishment. However, without repentance, they are all unprepared to meet Jesus at His coming. Their cry for admittance into the bridal chamber, "Lord, Lord, open to us," will be countermanded with the sad words, "**I never knew you**."

---

[3]Many of our musical entertainers who learned their first tunes in the Sunbeam band or little church choir, have now become instruments of Satan in the propagation of his diabolical, soul-destroying muck which is sweeping the world.

Not having the Spirit of Christ, their lives are tarnished with the works of the flesh: "Adultery, fornication, uncleanness, lasciviousness, Idolatry, witchcraft, hatred, variance, emulations, wrath, strife, seditions, heresies, Envyings, murders, drunkenness, revellings, and such like ..." (Galatians 5:19–21). For the most part, they have chosen "to enjoy the pleasures of sin for a season" rather than "to suffer affliction with the people of God" (Hebrews 11:25). They have not counted the worth of their souls, nor considered the vanity of the fleeting things of life.

Instead of making Christ the Lord of their lives, they have spurned His gracious love and guidance and gone their own willful ways. They have chosen "the pleasures of sin for a season," rather than the joy and blessedness of following in the footsteps of Jesus. They are building their lives upon the quicksands of what this world has to offer, rather than upon God's eternal values. These are the delinquent members found on all church rolls. They are servants of God in the sense that they give lip-service to the church program and even may participate in some of its religious activities, but their hearts are far from God and most of their waking hours are given over to materialistic interests and the gratification of their fleshly desires. "They profess that they know God; but in works they deny *him*, being abominable, and disobedient, and unto every good work reprobate" (Titus 1:16).

They are unfit for the kingdom of God and must be put through the fires of the Great Tribulation and brought to repentance and faith before being admitted into the portals of Heaven.

When the Rapture occurs, these spiritual delinquents will find themselves bereft of all they held dear. With the very heart and life of the church having disappeared from their midst, and most of their loved ones gone, they will realize the awful truth of the situation. They are left to the ruthlessness of a godless society and a wicked ruler who demands their obeisance to his image.

There is no describing the fate of those who are left behind and who refuse to bow down to the **image of the Beast** or receive **his mark**. Denied the right to buy or sell in the market places, they will be left to eke out a meager existence by begging and bartering their few belongings for daily sustenance. As social outcasts, they will be hounded, harassed, demeaned and persecuted, and forced to wander in the streets, the deserts, and the wastelands, suffering every deprivation known to man. For the majority there will be no escaping the Antichrist and his henchmen, who will finally overtake them and bring them under the sword of the executioner.

But this is not the end—God's mercy "endureth unto all generations," and He has promised that during this particular period in world history, "whosoever shall call on the name of the LORD shall be delivered [saved]" (Joel 2:30–32; Acts 2:19–21). In keeping with His promise, He will extend the hand of mercy to all who refuse the mark of the Beast and cry out to Him in faith and repentance. And although they still must suffer persecution and martyrdom under the cruel hand of the Antichrist (Revelation 13:15), they will escape the eternal damnation of their souls.

These unprofitable servants who have squandered [4] their lives, their time, talents, and possessions on worldly pleasures

---

[4]This is the meaning of hiding one's talent in the earth, rather than using it for God's glory.

and pursuits (Matthew 25:14–30) will make up a large part of the Tribulation saints of Revelation 6:9–11; 7:9–17. They are an innumerable company of Gentiles from all nations and kindreds, and peoples and tongues (Revelation 7:9), and although they will not be resurrected until the end of the Tribulation period, they are considered a part of the first resurrection and will take part in the millennial reign of Christ (Revelation 20:4–6).

However, they will never be a part of the raptured group but are a separate entity, with a different destiny. Whereas, the bride of Christ will have a personal, intimate relationship with Him and will share in His inheritance as kings and priests, the Tribulation saints will be servants in the temple of God, serving Him night and day.

Even so, God will reward them for their faithfulness to Him in refusing to bow down to the Antichrist or receive his mark. They will be given eternal life and will experience perfect bliss in heaven with Him for,

> "They shall hunger no more, neither thirst any more; neither shall the sun light on them, nor any heat. For the Lamb which is in the midst of the throne shall feed them, and shall lead them unto living fountains of waters: and God shall wipe away all tears from their eyes" (Revelation 7:16, 17).

Chapter 20
ISRAEL'S INHERITANCE

Israel is still living in anticipation of the appearance of her promised **Messiah**, the anointed King of Glory (Psalm 24:7–10), and the establishment of her earthly kingdom of peace and righteousness. Furthermore, she has every right under heaven to believe that her hopes will be realized, for the Old Testament is literally teeming with unfulfilled prophecies concerning these promises, and God has covenanted with an oath to bring them to pass.

> "Behold, the days come, saith the LORD, that I will perform that good thing which I have promised unto the house of Israel and to the house of Judah. In those days, and at that time, will I cause the Branch of righteousness to grow up unto David; and he shall execute judgment and righteousness in the land. In those days shall Judah be saved, and Jerusalem shall dwell safely: and this *is the name* wherewith she shall be called, The LORD our righteousness" (Jeremiah 33:14–16).

> "In that day will I raise up the tabernacle of David that is fallen, and close up the breaches thereof; and I will raise up his ruins, and I will build it as in the days of old: And I will bring again the captivity of my

> people of Israel, and they shall build the waste cities, and inhabit *them* … And I will plant them upon their land, and they shall no more be pulled up out of their land which I have given them, saith the LORD thy God" (Amos 9:11, 14, 15).

> "… I will gather them out of all countries, whither I have driven them … and I will bring them again unto this place, and I will cause them to dwell safely: And they shall be my people, and I will be their God …" (Jeremiah 32:37, 38).

> "… and I will save the house of Joseph, and I will bring them again to place them; for I have mercy upon them: and they shall be as though I had not cast them off: for I *am* the LORD their God, and will hear them" (Zechariah 10:6).

> "… a King shall reign and prosper, and shall execute judgment and justice in the earth. In his days Judah shall be saved, and Israel shall dwell safely …" (Jeremiah 23:5, 6).

God first made the promise to Abraham, when He called him out of the idolatrous city of Ur of the Chaldees, to go into a strange land and become the father of a new nation.

> "And the LORD said unto Abram … Lift up now thine eyes, and look from the place where thou art northward, and southward, and eastward, and westward: For all the land which thou seest, to thee

> will I give it, and to thy seed for ever" (Genesis 13:14, 15).

The LORD made a covenant with Abram, saying, "Unto thy seed have I given this land, from the river of Egypt unto the great river, the river Euphrates …" (Genesis 15:18).

> "And I will establish my covenant between me and thee and thy seed after thee in their generations for an everlasting covenant … And I will give unto thee, and to thy seed after thee, the land wherein thou art a stranger, all the land of Canaan, for an everlasting possession; and I will be their God" (Genesis 17:7, 8).

> "That in blessing I will bless thee, and in multiplying I will multiply thy seed as the stars of the heaven, and as the sand which *is* upon the sea shore; and thy seed shall possess the gate of his enemies; And in thy seed shall all the nations of the earth be blessed …" (Genesis 22:17, 18).

Some 800 years later, the covenant was renewed and confirmed to David, God's anointed king of Judah and a direct descendant of Abraham:

> "Thus saith the LORD of hosts … I will appoint a place for my people Israel, and will plant them, that they may dwell in a place of their own, and move no more; neither shall the children of wickedness afflict them any more, as beforetime … And when thy days be fulfilled, and thou shalt sleep with thy fathers, I will

> set up thy seed after thee, which shall proceed out of thy bowels, and I will establish his kingdom. He shall build an house for my name, and I will stablish the throne of his kingdom for ever … And thine house and thy kingdom ... thy throne shall be established for ever" (2 Samuel 7:8, 10–16).

The Lord has sworn by His holiness to keep this covenant with David:

> "My covenant will I not break, nor alter the thing that is gone out of my lips. Once have I sworn by my holiness that I will not lie unto David. His seed shall endure for ever, and his throne as the sun before me. It shall be established for ever as the moon …" (Psalm 89:34–37).

To break this covenant would require a power greater than the laws of nature governing night and day (Jeremiah 31:35–37). Thus, its fulfillment is as certain as the continued omnipotence of **Almighty God.**

In every generation of Jewish history, God has reserved unto Himself a remnant who have not bowed their knees to Baal and through whom He has preserved a spiritual posterity. In Elijah's day, there were 7,000 who had not bowed down to false gods (1 Kings 19:18, Romans 11:4). In Isaiah's time it was a "very small remnant" (Isaiah 1:9). When Jesus was born, the remnant was composed of "all them that looked for redemption in Jerusalem" (Luke 2:38). In Paul's day, it was "a remnant according to the election of grace" (Romans 11:5). Today, this remnant is scattered throughout the world, known only to the mind of God. Revelation 7:1–8 tells us that 144,000 Jews will be sealed with the "seal of the living God" at the beginning of the Tribulation as a protection against any or all forces that would destroy them, thus preserving them for eternity.

> "I say then, Hath God cast away his people? God forbid … God hath not cast away his people which he foreknew … Even so then at this present time also there is a remnant according to the election of grace … and the rest were blinded … I say then, Have they stumbled that they should fall? God forbid: but *rather* through their fall salvation *is come* unto the Gentiles … For if the casting away of them *be* the reconciling of the world, what *shall* the receiving *of them be*, but life from the dead? … because of unbelief they were broken off … if they abide not still in unbelief, shall be graffed in: for God is able to graff them in again … blindness in part is happened to Israel, until the fulness of the Gentiles be come in. And so all Israel shall be saved [that is, all who are living at the time of Christ's appearing] … For this *is* my covenant unto them, when I shall take away their sins" (Romans 11:1, 2, 5, 7, 11, 15, 20, 25–27).

God is not finished with Israel. Even though she has been unfaithful and is guilty of crucifying His Anointed One, He has not abandoned her as a nation and will yet work out His eternal purposes in and through this remnant, which has remained true to God and His **Christ.** This remnant constitutes a **spiritual Israel** within the national Israel, a remnant **according** to the **election of grace,** and the upshoot of these branches is being reserved for the great regathering at the time of Christ's return to set up His kingdom. God has not cast away His people—they will rise again. They are still the **people** of the **covenant,** and God will not fail to keep His word with them. He will bring them back into the **bond of the covenant** and cleanse and purify them, not for any merit on their part, but because He called them and separated them to fulfill a special mission in His program for eternity. But Israel **must repent,** and she **will repent** in unison when Christ appears in the heavens with the nail prints clearly visible in His hands and feet (Zechariah 13:6).

A great earthquake will split the Mount of Olives right through the center as Jesus descends to its summit, and the people will flee in all directions as they behold His glory.

> "And his feet shall stand in that day upon the mount of Olives, which *is* before Jerusalem on the east, and the mount of Olives shall cleave in the midst thereof toward the east and toward the west, *and there shall be* a very great valley; and half of the mountain shall remove toward the north, and half of it toward the south … and the LORD my God shall come, *and* all the saints with thee" (Zechariah 14:4, 5).

> "… and they shall look upon me whom they have pierced, and they shall mourn for him, as one mourneth for *his* only *son*, and shall be in bitterness for him, as one that is in bitterness for *his* firstborn" (Zechariah 12:10).

> "And *one* shall say unto him, What *are* these wounds in thine hands? Then he shall answer, *Those* with which I was wounded *in* the house of my friends" (Zechariah 13:6).

Together, they will exclaim: "Lo, this *is* our God; we have waited for him, and he will save us: this *is* the LORD … we will be glad and rejoice in his salvation" (Isa. 25:9). There has never in all the history of the world been such a homecoming as Israel will experience at the time of Jesus' return. In Matthew 24:30, 31 we read:

> "And then shall appear the sign of the Son of man in heaven: and then shall all the tribes of the earth mourn, and they shall see the Son of man coming in the clouds of heaven with power and great glory. And he shall send his angels with a great sound of a trumpet, and they shall gather together his elect from the four winds, from one end of heaven to the other."

From all directions they will come, as borne upon eagle's wings, to rejoice in their newly found Savior and to receive their eternal inheritance, which was allotted to them over 3,000 years ago (Joshua 15).

Chapter 21
ISRAEL'S PLIGHT

The history of Jerusalem sounds like a broken record:

Besieged—Ransacked—Desecrated—Burned—Conquered.
Besieged—Ransacked—Desecrated—Burned—Conquered.

Dating from the ninth century BC, when **Jerusalem** became the **capital** and **worship center** of **Israel**, down through the first century AD, the "**City of Peace**" had experienced little actual peace. Overwhelming national calamities were her portion from the very beginning as tribe after tribe of her warring neighbors laid siege to her valuable possessions. Portions of her walls were repeatedly broken down, her **holy temple** and palaces plundered and stripped of their sacred vessels and costly array, and her people were taken captive into heathen territories.

God had chosen Israel out of a world of idolatry for a very special mission on the earth. She was to be a witness for Him—a lighthouse in the midst of sin and spiritual darkness and an example of what a nation would be if wholly committed to doing His will. She was to point the way to the coming **Messiah** and, finally, her nation was to bring forth that Messiah and present Him to the world as the **only begotten Son of God** and **Savior** of mankind.

But Israel played the **harlot**. Instead of bearing testimony to the greatness and goodness of the **One True God**, she forsook Him and went a whoring after the Canaanite people and their false gods. In disobedience to God's commandment to exterminate these wicked, unrepentant nations, they intermarried with them and indulged in their shameful, heathen rituals, including their abominable fertility (sex) rites. They practiced divination and enchantments, built altars to Baal, Ashtaroth, and other false gods, and burned their sons and daughters as sin offerings.

God sent prophet after prophet to warn them of the consequences, but they mocked and misused them and continually "did evil in the sight of the Lord" until they provoked Him to anger and sealed their own doom. By way of chastisement, God repeatedly delivered them into the hands of their enemies. Occasionally, they would cry out to Him for deliverance and were rescued over and over again by His persistent love and mercy.

Continued disobedience led to internal confusion and division of the kingdom (1 Kings 12:16, 17). Then, finally came the Assyrian and Babylonian captivities, which ended in the complete destruction of the city of Jerusalem by Nebuchadnezzar in 598 BC. Millions of Jews were uprooted from their homeland and led away captive into the distant, strange lands of Babylonia, leaving their beloved, once-glorious "City of Peace" a pile of rubbish.

Partial restorations of the walls and temple worship were made following the captivities, but marauding bands continued to besiege her fortifications and molest her people during the centuries following. The Persians, the Greeks, the Ptolemies and Seleucids, the Syrians, and the Parthians, all took their turn at despoiling the holy city, so that Israel never again regained her former glory, nor did she ever possess the Promised Land in all of its entirety. Eventually, in 37 BC, all former Jewish territories were swallowed up by the Roman Empire, and Judea became a vassal of the Roman government under the dynasty of the Herods, who rebuilt the city and the temple on a magnificent scale in keeping with Grecian architecture.

These were the conditions under which Jesus was born in Bethlehem of Judea, in the reign of Herod the Great. The birth of Jesus to the virgin Mary came after many centuries of waiting and anticipation on the part of the Jewish people. Yet, when He came in the role of the **suffering Servant** (Isa. 53), they refused to accept Him as their **Messiah**. Even though He came announcing the **kingdom of heaven** "at hand," and proved His identity by many signs and wonders, yet the Jewish leaders put Him down as a rank imposter, and would have no part of Him.

Consequently, He announced that the kingdom of God would be taken from them and given to a nation that would accept Him through faith and bring forth fruits to His glory, i.e., the **Gentiles** (Matthew 21:43).

> "He was in the world, and the world was made by him, and the world knew him not. He came unto his own [the Jewish race], and his own received him not (John 1:10, 11).

Instead of receiving the blessed Savior into their hearts as **Messiah** and **King**, they turned Him over to the Roman authorities with the suicidal cry, "Crucify *him*, crucify him" (Luke 23:21). "His blood *be* on us, and on our children" (Matthew 27:25).

A few days before the final rejection, Jesus looking out over the city of Jerusalem, predicted her destruction.

> "O Jerusalem, Jerusalem, *thou* that killest the prophets, and stonest them which are sent unto thee, how often would I have gathered thy children together, even as a hen gathereth her chickens under *her* wings, and ye would not! Behold, your house is left unto you desolate" (Matthew 23:37, 38).

The final blow came in AD 70 when an uprising of the Jews prompted Titus to wipe out the city completely. The attack was staged during the week of the Passover feast, when 3,000,000 Jews were packed and jammed within its city walls.

According to Josephas, over 1,000,000 Jews died in the holocaust. Six hundred thousand of these starved to death, and hundreds of others, threatened with starvation, were massacred by their own kinsmen. A torch thrown inadvertently over the wall set fire to the entire city, once more reducing it to a pile of rubbish. Thousands were taken captive, and those who escaped took refuge in the caves near the Dead Sea, later to become once again scattered throughout the Gentile nations of the world.

Chapter 22

ISRAELITES VERSUS MUSLIMS

For almost nineteen centuries, God's chosen people remained scattered like grains of sand in the wind, with no organized government and no place to call their own. Then, "Presto!" the seemingly impossible happened!

On May 14, 1948, Palestine was declared an independent state under the Balfour Declaration and partitioned between Israel and Jordan (Palestinian Arabs). Since then, a constant stream of Jews have returned to their homeland and, once again, they have been restored to their national identity.

However, Israel has not even begun to tap the potential God intended for her future. Out of an estimated 20,000,000 Jews worldwide, less than 3,000,000 have migrated to their homeland, leaving the bulk of their population scattered throughout the Gentile world where they are often subjected to bitter hatred and persecution. Almost 3,000,000 still reside within the Communist block.

Although Israel's borders were extended in the Six-Day War to include all of Jerusalem, the West Bank, and the Gaza Strip, most of the territory promised Abraham's seed is still unclaimed and unpossessed. When possessed in all its entirety, it will extend from the Euphrates River southward to the River of Egypt, including all of Lebanon and the western half of Syria.

During the almost 2,000 years in which the Jews were absent from their homeland, the Muslim Arabs had become entrenched there. As a result of Israel's return, some 70,000 Arabs whose ancestors had lived in Palestine for centuries, have been uprooted and forced to find refuge in surrounding countries, where they are unwanted and unwelcome. Still, many Arabs remain in Jewish territory to haunt them night and day by their very presence.

To deepen Israel's resentment and shame, and to add to her reproach, the Muslim shrine, the Mosque of Omar, sits squarely upon the old temple site and prevents the rebuilding of her own beloved temple and the establishment of her ancient religious rites.

These two nations have been bitter enemies from the earliest days of Jewish history. Both are direct descendants of Abraham, but both are not equal when it comes to God's covenant with their father, Abraham (Genesis 17:1–8). The **Arabs** are descendants of **Ishmael**, the illegitimate son of Abraham by the Egyptian bondwoman, **Hagar**. He is the product of Abraham's unbelief and rash behavior. None of the covenant blessings belong to his posterity.

The **Israelites** (Jews) are descendants of **Isaac**, the only son of Abraham and his wife, Sarah. He is the "son of promise," and all of the covenants God made with Abraham are to be fulfilled in and through his posterity. The land, the blessings, and the spiritual seed (through Christ) all belong to **Isaac**, and therefore, to the Jewish nation (Genesis 16–18 and 21).

Every confrontation that erupts between the Muslims and the Jews is but another skirmish in the age-old quarrel over the rights of **Ishmael and Isaac**. Both nations are well aware of the covenant promises, but both are intent upon possessing the land. So, the feud goes on, even to this day.

However, the question was settled centuries ago when Abraham pled for Ishmael to have part in the covenant promises, and God answered him:

> "And as for Ishmael, I have heard thee: Behold, I have blessed him, and will make him fruitful, and will multiply him exceedingly; twelve princes shall he beget, and I will make him a great nation. But my covenant will I establish with Isaac, which Sarah shall bear unto thee …" (Genesis 17:20, 21).

Today, Israel sits as in olden times, on a little plot of ground in the midst of a nest of hostile nations, all of whom would obliterate her from the face of the earth if they could. With the Palestinian Arabs to her back; Egypt and Saudi Arabia to the South; Iraq, Iran, Syria and war-torn Lebanon to the North, and oil-hungry Russia hovering over all, ready to pounce upon any who stand in her way to the Persian Gulf—little Israel is indeed in a precarious position!

There is no rest for Israel. With 700,000,000 Muslims demanding that Jerusalem be returned to them, she stands armed to the hilt with stockpiles of ultra-modern weapons, and guns cocked in every direction, ready to fire at the least provocation.

There is one thing to her credit. She believes God's promises and will not let go of His covenant blessings. She is prepared to fight to the finish to protect her precious inheritance and to assure the world of a continued posterity to occupy it. But, is this God's way, to have His chosen people **fight** for the right to occupy a territory which He has already assigned to them? Is God in this thing at all, or is it, as usual, the result of man's blundering?

It is both. God is in everything in the sense that He permits events and circumstances to occur. He is all powerful and nothing can happen unless He permits it. Israel is in God's **permissive will**. She must suffer the consequences of her wrongdoing. Her greatest sin is the rejection of the Messiah to whom she gave birth.

The lovely Son of God who was in the beginning with God and equal with God, left all of the riches of heaven and condescended to take upon Himself the form of a man, even to becoming the servant of man (Philippians 2:6–8). He was gracious, humble, kind and compassionate. He lived and walked among His kinsmen and neighbors for thirty-three years, a life of sinless perfection, proving Himself to be God by "many infallible proofs" (Acts 1:3). But His humility and graciousness were revolting to the Jewish leaders, and they would have no part of Him. When He made a public offer of Himself as King of Israel, both the leaders and the multitudes hailed Him as the "Prophet of Nazareth," but only a handful acknowledged Him as the true Messiah, whom He really was.

This is Israel's great sin today. "They are turned back to the iniquities of their forefathers" (Jeremiah 11:10), and nothing short of the most severe chastisement will bring them to repentance. They still acknowledge Jesus as a prophet of Israel but have never received Him into their hearts as the Son of God and the Saviour of the world. Although they proclaim long and loud their undying faith in God's covenant blessings, yet they have rejected the living Christ, the very one through whom they were to have received their blessings.

For the sins of the forefathers, then, the Jewish nation is **blind** and **deaf** to all New Testament revelations concerning her **Messiah** (Isaiah 6:9–11; Matthew 13:13, 15; Romans

11:25). For her obstinate rejection of the Son of God as her promised **Messiah**, she remains dispersed and hated and persecuted throughout the world today. Yet her present affliction is but a foreshadow of that which is to come, for "I send thee … to a rebellious nation … For *they are* impudent children and stiffhearted …" (Ezekiel 2:3–5).

Just as God in His fury and hatred for their sins, scattered them among the nations of the earth, so does He propose to bring them through the crucible and into the bond of the covenant, which He made with their forefathers. Many Scriptures express His determination to do this:

> "… the house of Israel is to me become dross … Therefore thus saith the Lord GOD; Because ye are all become dross, behold, therefore … I will gather you, and blow upon you in the fire of my wrath, and ye shall be melted in the midst thereof. As silver is melted in the midst of the furnace, so shall ye be melted in the midst thereof; and ye shall know that I the LORD have poured out my fury upon you" (Ezekiel 22:18–22).

> "*As* I live, saith the Lord GOD, surely with a mighty hand, and with a stretched out arm, and with fury poured out, will I rule over you: And I will bring you out from the people, and will gather you out of the countries wherein ye are scattered … And I will cause you to pass under the rod, and I will bring you into the bond of the covenant … I will purge out from among you the rebels, and them that transgress against me …" (Ezekiel 20:33, 34, 37, 38).

> "All the sinners of my people shall die by the sword, which say, The evil shall not overtake nor prevent us" (Amos 9:10).

> "And it shall come to pass, *that* in all the land … two parts therein shall be cut off *and* die; but the third shall be left therein. And I will bring the third part through the fire, and will refine them as silver is refined, and will try them as gold is tried: they shall call on my name, and I will hear them: I will say, It *is* my people: and they shall say, The LORD *is* my God" (Zechariah 13:8, 9).

These Scriptures were partially fulfilled in the siege of Titus in AD 70, but they definitely point to a future judgment, for although Israel has passed through the fire of God's judgment countless times, she has never been purified and brought into **"the bond of the covenant"** (Ezekiel 20:37), which the Lord made with her. The Great Tribulation is distinctly the "time of Jacob's [Israel's] trouble," and all events leading up to its climax, center in and around Jerusalem. Thus, it is here in the land of her nativity that she is to be purged of her sins.

There has been a gradual returning of the Jews to the land of their forefathers since the first World War, and this is now being intensified under the Zionist Movement. However, the greatest movement of returning Jews will be in response to a mandate from the Antichrist to rebuild their temple and renew their religious ceremonies and sacrifices.

This will be accomplished at the beginning of his evil reign, but in the middle of the week (halfway into the

Tribulation), he will break the covenant, cause the "sacrifice and oblation" to cease, and set himself up in the temple, declaring himself to be God (2 Thessalonians 2:3, 4). When they resist his overtures, he will turn on them and seek to annihilate the whole Jewish race.

This is the beginning of events leading up to the Battle of Armageddon and the final destruction of Gentile world powers. It is probably the point where Russia (Gog and Magog of Ezek. 38) comes down from the North to claim her share of the spoils. At any rate, the entire world will become embroiled in conflict over the little Jewish nation. God's word says:

> "For, lo, I will call all the families of the kingdoms of the north … and they shall come, and they shall set every one his throne at the entering of the gates of Jerusalem, and against all the walls thereof round about, and against all the cities of Judah" (Jeremiah 1:15).

> "For I will gather all nations against Jerusalem to battle; and the city shall be taken, and the houses rifled, and the women ravished; and half of the city shall go forth into captivity, and the residue of the people shall not be cut off from the city" (Zechariah 14:2).

> "Behold, I will make Jerusalem a cup of trembling unto all the people round about, when they shall be in the siege both against Judah *and* against Jerusalem … And it shall come to pass in that day, *that* I will seek to destroy all the nations that come against Jerusalem" (Zechariah 12:2, 9).

Just as everything seems hopeless for Israel, the Lord Jesus Christ will suddenly appear through the open heavens, with an army of mobilized saints and angels to smite the nations and take over the reins of government (Revelation 19:1–16; Zechariah 14:4, 5). When He appears, the escaping remnant will acknowledge Him as their **LORD** and **SAVIOUR**, for "the LORD *will be* the hope of his people, and the strength of the children of Israel" (Joel 3:16).

> "And it shall be said in that day, Lo, this *is* our God; we have waited for him, and he will save us: this *is* the LORD … we will be glad and rejoice in his salvation" (Isaiah 25:9).

Yes, Israel has every right under heaven to look for her promised Messiah, but a great shock is in store for her people when they are made to realize that **He** is the **One** whom they rejected and crucified.

Even now, in blindness and unbelief—still rejecting Jesus as their Messiah, and oblivious to the dangers ahead—the Jews are being coaxed into Palestine at the rate of 10,000 a year, wholly unaware of the plight that awaits them.

> "For they *are* a nation void of counsel, neither *is there any* understanding in them. O that they were wise, *that* they understood this, *that* they would consider their latter end!" (Deuteronomy 32:28, 29).

Chapter 23
CHRIST'S REIGN ON EARTH

All the world events are moving toward the one great pivotal point in God's program for the ages, the **return of Christ** in **power and glory**, to put down His adversaries and begin the setting up of His own **righteous reign**. Both the Old and New Testament prophets describe the redeemed and recreated earth in glowing terms, and men of every age have longed to see their fulfillment.

Daniel had a vision in which he beheld the **Ancient of Days** (God) sitting upon a throne:

> "A fiery stream issued and came forth from before him: thousand thousands ministered unto him, and ten thousand times ten thousand stood before him: the judgment was set, and the books were opened … and, behold, *one* like the Son of man came with the clouds of heaven, and came to the Ancient of days, and they brought him near before him. And there was given him dominion, and glory, and a kingdom, that all people, nations, and languages, should serve him: his dominion *is* an everlasting dominion, which shall not pass away, and his kingdom *that* which shall not be destroyed … And the kingdom and dominion, and the greatness of the kingdom under the whole heaven, shall be given to the people of the saints of the most

> High, whose kingdom *is* an everlasting kingdom, and all dominions shall serve and obey him" (Daniel 7:10, 13, 14, 27).

Zechariah, Isaiah, and Jeremiah give a more detailed description of the coming **King** and His **Kingdom**:

> "And it shall be in that day, *that* living waters shall go out from Jerusalem; half of them toward the former sea, and half of them toward the hinder sea: in summer and in winter shall it be. And the LORD shall be king over all the earth: in that day shall there be one LORD, and his name one" (Zechariah 14:8, 9).

> "… and the government shall be upon his shoulder: and his name shall be called Wonderful, Counsellor, The mighty God, The everlasting Father, The Prince of Peace. Of the increase of *his* government and peace *there shall be* no end, upon the throne of David, and upon his kingdom, to order it, and to establish it with judgment and with justice from henceforth even for ever" (Isaiah 9:6, 7).

> "And it shall come to pass in the last days, *that* the mountain of the LORD'S house shall be established in the top of the mountains, and shall be exalted above the hills; and all nations shall flow unto it. And many people shall go and say, Come ye, and let us go up to the mountain of the LORD, to the house of the God of Jacob; and he will teach us of his ways, and we will walk in his paths: for out of Zion shall go forth

> the law, and the word of the LORD from Jerusalem. And he shall judge among the nations, and shall rebuke many people: and they shall beat their swords into plowshares, and their spears into pruninghooks: nation shall not lift up sword against nation, neither shall they learn war any more" (Isaiah 2:2–4).

Christ has yet to sit upon the "Throne of Glory" and reign over the earth in the fullness of His power. Also, Israel is destined to reach the zenith of her power during His glorious reign, with David serving as prince regent under Christ, and the twelve apostles sitting on their individual thrones judging the twelve tribes of Israel (Ezekiel 34:24; Matthew 19:29).

The city of Jerusalem is to be the center of the earth's activities during the millennial reign (Isaiah 2:2–4). Here, Christ will sit upon the throne of His father, David, during His frequent appearances upon the earth, and all flesh will be gathered to see His glory and to worship before Him (Isaiah 66:18–23).

> "And it shall come to pass, *that* every one that is left of all the nations which came against Jerusalem shall even go up from year to year to worship the King, the LORD of hosts, and to keep the feast of tabernacles" (Zechariah 14:16).

> "... Again there shall be heard in this place, which ye say *shall be* desolate without man and without beast ... The voice of joy, and the voice of gladness, the voice of the bridegroom, and the voice of the bride, the voice of them that shall say, Praise the LORD of

> hosts: for the LORD *is* good; for his mercy *endureth* for ever …" (Jeremiah 33:10, 11).

> "The wolf also shall dwell with the lamb, and the leopard shall lie down with the kid; and the calf and the young lion and the fatling together; and a little child shall lead them. And the cow and the bear shall feed; their young ones shall lie down together: and the lion shall eat straw like the ox. And the sucking child shall play on the hole of the asp, and the weaned child shall put his hand on the cockatrice' den. They shall not hurt nor destroy in all my holy mountain: for the earth shall be full of the knowledge of the LORD, as the waters cover the sea" (Isaiah 11:6–9).

Try to visualize the earth, free from satanic influence and domination—void of impurities and everything of a destructive nature. No sorrow, no strife, no want, no fear—even the heavens will be cleansed of all evil and rebellious spirits, and the whole earth will be filled with joy, praise, peace and beauty.

This is the glorious habitation, which God has covenanted to establish on earth under the reign of His Only Begotten Son, and although there has been a delay of some 6,000 years, God is not to be prevented from carrying out His desired purpose for His earthly creation. "But he *is* in one *mind*, and who can turn him? and *what* his soul desireth, even *that* he doeth" (Job 23:13).

The whole land was desolate when God planted the Garden of Eden and placed man in it. He gave him the power and the wisdom to subdue and develop the entire earth and commanded him to do so. But Satan entered the scene, and man fell victim to his power, thereby becoming an instrument through which Satan began his tireless efforts to regain control of the earth.

However, we find that after 6,000 years of Satan's untiring activities in an effort to rebuild his kingdom, he is to end his menacing career by making the whole earth desolate again and landing in the bottomless pit (Revelation 20:3).

With Satan in the pit and his kingdom destroyed, the Spirit of the Lord will be manifest in all the earth, eventually making it into a veritable **paradise**. And they shall say,

> "… This land that was desolate is become like the garden of Eden; and the waste and desolate and ruined cities *are become* fenced, *and* are inhabited … I the LORD have spoken *it*, and I will do *it*" (Ezekiel 36:35, 36).

> "And the LORD shall be king over all the earth: in that day shall there be one LORD, and his name one" (Zechariah 14:9).

It should be remembered that although the whole earth will be laid waste during the Tribulation period, all of its inhabitants will not be destroyed. It is true that God determines to make a full end of all nations except Israel, but it is their present world systems that are to be destroyed, rather than the entire human race.

How some will escape the wrath of the Antichrist is not known, but most likely they are the poor, the meek and the lowly, living in the remote sections of the world, who pose no threat to his power. These will make up God's remnant through whom He will perpetuate the Gentile race, fulfilling Jesus' promise: "Blessed *are* the meek: for they shall inherit the earth" (Matthew 5:5).

With these remaining Gentiles, the Jewish remnant, and all of the resurrected Old Testament saints, the rehabilitation of the earth and the restoration of the Davidic kingdom will begin under the supervision of the King of Glory and His glorified bride. The great work of rehabilitation will begin at Jerusalem, the city of the great King (Matthew 5:35), for which complete specifications have already been drawn (Ezekiel 40–43), and from there it will reach out to the uttermost parts of the earth. With millions of both Old and New Testament saints in their glorified bodies, and under perfect regimentation, they will be able to function at top speed. Also, fast modes of travel will be available to those still in the flesh, and the work will progress at a rapid rate.

The curse, under which all creation has groaned and travailed for 6,000 years, will be lifted and the entire earth will blossom forth with a profusion of plant life, such as human eyes have never beheld.

> "… the desert shall rejoice, and blossom as the rose. It shall blossom abundantly, and rejoice even with joy and singing …" (Isaiah 35:1, 2).

Climatic and atmospheric conditions will be perfect, with rains in due season to bring abundant crops. There will be no more floods, earthquakes, tornadoes, hurricanes, electrical storms—all will be peace and quiet.

> "Then the eyes of the blind shall be opened, and the ears of the deaf shall be unstopped. Then shall the lame *man* leap as an hart, and the tongue of the dumb sing: for in the wilderness shall waters break out, and streams in the desert. And the parched ground shall become a pool, and the thirsty land springs of water … And the ransomed of the LORD shall return, and come to Zion with songs and everlasting joy upon their heads: they shall obtain joy and gladness, and sorrow and sighing shall flee away" (Isaiah 35:5–7, 10).

At the close of the 1,000-year reign of Christ, Satan will be loosed out of his prison for a "little season," and will make one final effort to overcome the power of God and His Christ. Vast armies will be mobilized from all parts of the world showing that their old natures have not changed, even though their desires have been suppressed and subdued under the iron rule of Christ (Revelation 19:15).

> "And they went up on the breadth of the earth, and compassed the camp of the saints about, and the beloved city [Jerusalem]: and fire came down from God out of heaven, and devoured them" (Revelation 20:9).

Following this, **Satan** is cast into the **Lake of Fire** where the Beast and False Prophet are, and will be "tormented day and night for ever and ever" (Revelation 20:10).

The Great White Throne then appears in heaven and the **wicked dead** are brought up from hell to face the **judgment of God.**

> "… and they were judged every man according to their works" (Revelation 20:13).
>
> "And whosoever was not found written in the book of life was cast into the lake of fire … the fearful, and unbelieving, and the abominable, and murderers, and whoremongers, and sorcerers, and idolaters, and all liars, shall have their part in the lake which burneth with fire and brimstone: which is the second death" (Revelation 20:15; 21:8).

Eternity follows this with the **new heaven** and the **new earth** taking the place of the old, and the **holy city**, new Jerusalem, coming down from God out of heaven:

> "And I saw a new heaven and a new earth: for the first heaven and the first earth were passed away; and there was no more sea. And I John saw the holy city, new Jerusalem, coming down from God out of heaven, prepared as a bride adorned for her husband. And I heard a great voice out of heaven saying, Behold, the tabernacle of God *is* with men, and he will dwell with them, and they shall be his people, and God himself shall be with them, *and be* their God. And God shall wipe away all tears from their eyes; and there shall be no more death, neither sorrow, nor crying, neither shall there be any more pain: for the former things are passed away. And he that sat upon the throne said, Behold, I make all things new. And he said unto me, Write: for these words are true and faithful. And he said unto me, It is done. I am Alpha and Omega, the

beginning and the end. I will give unto him that is athirst of the fountain of the water of life freely. He that overcometh shall inherit all things; and I will be his God, and he shall be my son" (Revelation 21:1–7).

"And there shall be no more curse: but the throne of God and of the Lamb shall be in it; and his servants shall serve him: And they shall see his face; and his name *shall be* in their foreheads. And there shall be no night there; and they need no candle, neither light of the sun; for the Lord God giveth them light: and they shall reign for ever and ever" (Revelation 22:3–5).

"Then *cometh* the end, when he shall have delivered up the kingdom to God, even the Father; when he shall have put down all rule and all authority and power. For he must reign, till he hath put all enemies under his feet. The last enemy *that* shall be destroyed *is* death. For he hath put all things under his feet. But when he saith all things are put under *him, it is* manifest that he is excepted, which did put all things under him. And when all things shall be subdued unto him, then shall the Son also himself be subject unto him that put all things under him, that God may be all in all" (1 Corinthians 15:24–28).

Chapter 24

GOD'S ULTIMATUMS

"Be still, and know that I *am* God... I will shake the heavens and the earth ... I will overthrow the throne of kingdoms ... I will be exalted among the heathen, I will be exalted in the earth" (Psalm 46:10; Haggai 2:21, 22).

The **Spirit** is striving with all mankind—**warning**, **pleading**, **reproving**, **admonishing**—

"... not willing that any should perish, but that all should come to repentance" (2 Peter 3:9).

"He that hath an ear, let him hear what the Spirit saith unto the churches ..." (Revelation 2:7).

"... behold, I come quickly; and my reward *is* with me, to give every man according as his work shall be" (Revelation 22:12).

"But ye, brethren, are not in darkness, that that day should overtake you as a thief. Ye are all the children of light, and the children of the day ... Therefore let us not sleep, as *do* others; but let us watch and be sober" (1 Thessalonians 5:4–6).

"Watch therefore: for ye know not what hour your Lord doth come … be ye also ready: for in such an hour as ye think not the Son of man cometh" (Matthew 24:42, 44).

"And take heed to yourselves, lest at any time your hearts be overcharged with surfeiting, and drunkenness, and cares of this life, and *so* that day come upon you unawares. For as a snare shall it come on all them that dwell on the face of the whole earth. Watch ye therefore, and pray always, that ye may be accounted worthy to escape all these things that shall come to pass, and to stand before the Son of man" (Luke 21:34–36).

Repent! **Watch**! **Wait**! and **Be Ready**! "… for that blessed hope, and the glorious appearing of the great God and our Saviour Jesus Christ … Lest coming suddenly he find you sleeping" (Titus 2:13; Mark 13:36).

TO THE FEARFUL AND UNBELIEVING:

"… the Lord Jesus shall be revealed from heaven with his mighty angels, In flaming fire taking vengeance on them that know not God, and that obey not the gospel of our Lord Jesus Christ: Who shall be punished with everlasting destruction from the presence of the Lord, and from the glory of his power …: (2 Thessalonians 1:7–9).

"As therefore the tares are gathered and burned in the fire; so shall it be in the end of this world. The Son of man shall send forth his angels, and they shall gather out of his kingdom all things that offend, and them which do iniquity; And shall cast them into a furnace of fire: there shall be wailing and gnashing of teeth" (Matthew 13:40–42).

"… do ye not know their tokens, That the wicked is reserved to the day of destruction? they shall be brought forth to the day of wrath" (Job 21:29, 30).

"Upon the wicked he shall rain snares, fire and brimstone, and an horrible tempest: *this shall be* the portion of their cup" (Psalm 11:6).

"But the fearful, and unbelieving, and the abominable, and murderers, and whoremongers, and sorcerers, and idolaters, and all liars, shall have their part in the lake which burneth with fire and brimstone: which is the second death" (Revelation 21:8).

"... *As* I live, saith the Lord GOD, I have no pleasure in the death of the wicked; but that the wicked turn from his way and live: turn ye, turn ye from your evil ways …" (Ezekiel 33:11).

"… Believe on the Lord Jesus Christ, and thou shalt be saved …" (Acts 16:31).

TO THE NATION OF ISRAEL:

"Behold, the eyes of the Lord GOD *are* upon the sinful kingdom, and I will destroy it from off the face of the earth; saving that I will not utterly destroy the house of Jacob …" (Amos 9:8).

"Therefore fear thou not, O my servant Jacob, saith the LORD; neither be dismayed, O Israel: for, lo, I will save thee from afar, and thy seed from the land of their captivity; and Jacob shall return, and shall be in rest, and be quiet, and none shall make *him* afraid. For I *am* with thee, saith the LORD, to save thee: though I make a full end of all nations whither I have scattered thee, yet will I not make a full end of thee: but I will correct thee in measure, and will not leave thee altogether unpunished … I have wounded thee with the wound of an enemy, with the chastisement of a cruel one, for the multitude of thine iniquity … *because* thy sins were increased, I have done these things unto thee" (Jeremiah 30:10, 11, 14, 15).

"*But* Israel shall be saved in the LORD with an everlasting salvation: ye shall not be ashamed nor confounded world without end" (Isaiah 45:17).

"For I will take you from among the heathen, and gather you out of all countries, and will bring you into your own land … And ye shall dwell in the land that I gave to your fathers; and ye shall be my people, and I will be your God" (Ezekiel 36:24, 28).

"… Turn ye again now every one from his evil way, and from the evil of your doings, and dwell in the land that the LORD hath given unto you and to your fathers for ever and ever" (Jeremiah 25:5).

"… Return unto me, and I will return unto you, saith the LORD of hosts" (Malachi 3:7).

TO THE WORLD AT LARGE:

"Look unto me, and be ye saved, all the ends of the earth: for I *am* God, and *there is* none else" (Isaiah 45:22).

"I am Alpha and Omega, the beginning and the ending … which is, and which was, and which is to come, the Almighty" (Revelation 1:8).

"… *I am* God, and *there is* none like me, Declaring the end from the beginning, and from ancient times *the things* that are not *yet* done, saying, My counsel shall stand, and I will do all my pleasure … yea, I have spoken *it*, I will also bring it to pass; I have purposed *it*, I will also do it" (Isaiah 46:9–11).

"For as the rain cometh down, and the snow from heaven, and returneth not thither, but watereth the earth, and maketh it bring forth and bud, that it may give seed to the sower, and bread to the eater: So shall my word be that goeth forth out of my mouth: it shall not return unto me void, but it shall accomplish that which I please, and it shall prosper *in the thing* whereto I sent it" (Isaiah 55:10, 11).

"… I *am* the LORD: I will speak, and the word that I shall speak shall come to pass; it shall be no more prolonged …" (Ezekiel 12:25).

"… that that is determined shall be done" (Daniel 11:36).

"Seek ye the LORD while he may be found, call ye upon him while he is near …" (Isaiah 55:6).

"For what *is* your life? It is even a vapour, that appeareth for a little time, and then vanisheth away" (James 4:14).

"For all flesh *is* as grass, and all the glory of man as the flower of grass. The grass withereth, and the flower thereof falleth away: But the word of the Lord endureth for ever" (1 Peter 1:24, 25).

"For all that *is* in the world, the lust of the flesh, and the lust of the eyes, and the pride of life, is not of the Father, but is of the world. And the world passeth away, and the lust thereof: but he that doeth the will of God abideth for ever" (1 John 2:16, 17).

Postscript

WHY JESUS MUST COME TO EARTH AGAIN?

First and foremost, He must come to earth again, **because He always keeps His word**! He said,

> "And if I go and prepare a place for you, I will come again, and receive you unto myself; that where I am, *there* ye may be also" (John 14:3).

The Word of God clearly states prophetically,

> "And the LORD shall be king over all the earth: in that day shall there be one LORD, and his name one." (Zechariah 14:9).

JESUS MUST COME:

...To deliver the righteous from the approaching holocaust that is coming upon all the world.

...To chain Satan and cast him into the bottomless pit, and finally into the Lake of Fire where he will burn forever.

...To vindicate the righteous by destroying the wicked from off the face of the earth.

...To destroy the Antichrist and the False Prophet, Satan's henchmen.

...To empty the hospitals, nursing homes and mental institutions.

...To heal the brokenhearted, raise the dead, give sight to the blind, hearing to the deaf, and healing to the sick and afflicted.

...To cleanse and purify the atmosphere in preparation for His kingdom of peace and righteousness.

...To lift the curse and replace it with a perfect environment.

...To put an end to all of His enemies, including death, which is the last enemy to be destroyed.

...To fulfill all of His promises concerning the establishment of a peaceful and righteous world order.

...To bring mankind back to God's original plan and purpose as is seen in the garden before sin. The circle will be completed, and man will once again live in perfect harmony with God, in a perfect environment, serving a perfect Saviour!

Postscript

SIGNS OF JESUS' SOON RETURN

1. Man's wickedness and lawlessness (Romans 1:18–32).
2. The multiple increase of earthquakes, volcanic eruptions, hurricanes, tornadoes, pestilences, famines and plagues (Matthew 24:3–24; Luke 21:11).
3. Wars, fightings and general unrest (Matthew 24:6, 7).
4. Signs in the sun, moon, and stars, bringing changes in weather conditions (Luke 21:25, 26).
5. Distress of nations with perplexities (Luke 21:25).
6. Men's hearts failing them for fear (Luke 21:26).
7. False christs, false prophets and false doctrines (Matthew 24:5; 1 Tim. 4:1; 1 John 4:1–3).
8. The accumulation of wealth by the few (James 5:1–6).
9. The return of the Jews to their homeland (Ezekiel 36:24).
10. Persecution of the Jews (Luke 21:12–17).
11. Mockers who scoff at any mention of the second coming of Christ (2 Peter 3:3, 4).
12. Apostasy of the church (Revelation 3:16).
13. A pleasure-seeking world (2 Timothy 3:4).
14. Man's intervention into space and his evil inventions and imaginations (Romand 1:30; Genesis 6:5; Isaiah 14:13–15).
15. People running to and fro and increasing knowledge (Daniel 12:4).
16. The promise of peace by politicians and religios leaders (1 Thessalonians 5:3).

17. Perilous times upon every nation of the globe (2 Timothy 3:1).

"when ye shall see these things, know that it is near, *even* at the doors. Verily I say unto you, This generation [the generation that sees these signs] shall not pass, till all these things be fulfilled" (Matthew 24:33, 34).

Postscript

DIFFERENCES IN THE TWO COMINGS

The first time He came as a Lamb (John 1:29); the next time He'll come as a Lion (Amos 3:8; Revelation 5:5).

The first time, He came with grace and truth (John 1:17); the next time He'll come with vengeance and wrath (Revelation 6:17).

The first time, He came to a stable (Luke 2:7); the next time He'll come to a throne (Matthew 19:28).

The first time, He rode a mule into Jerusalem (John 12:15); the next time He'll be riding a white stallion (Revelation 19:11).

The first time, He wore a crown of thorns (Matthew 27:29); the next time He'll wear many crowns (Revelation 19:12).

The first time, He came to die (Mark 8:31); the next time He'll come to kill (Revelation 16).

The first time, He came to serve (John 13); the next time He'll come to be served (Revelation 22:3).

Yes, **THE KING IS COMING**! Are **YOU** ready?